A GIRDLE ROUND THE EARTH

D1556613

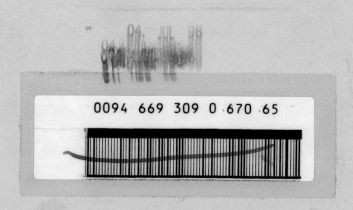

A GIRDLE ROUND THE EARTH

MARIA AITKEN

Captions, pictures and additional research
PETER KING

Constable · London

First published in Great Britain 1987
by Constable and Company Limited
10 Orange Street London WC2H 7EG
Copyright © 1987 by Maria Aitken
set in Monophoto Baskerville 11 pt
and printed in Great Britain by
BAS Printers Ltd, Over Wallop
Designed by Tom Sawyer

British Library CIP data
Aitken, Maria
    A girdle round the earth.
    1. Voyages and travels   2. Travellers,
    Women – History
    I. Title
    910′.88042   G465

ISBN 0 09 466930 9

To my adventurous mother,
Penelope Aitken

ACKNOWLEDGEMENTS

I would like to thank Peter King for his additional research and picture research for the book, and also for his advice and suggestions generally which have contributed to the final text. I would also like to thank Caroline Keely for her boundless enthusiasm and her help with research, Nathan Silver for his encouragement and for his intolerance of sloppy punctuation, and Margaret Forrester for typing my manuscript. Miss Alexandra Allen of the RGS has very kindly checked the text for inaccuracies, and Robin Baird-Smith and Prudence Fay of Constable have persuaded me onwards with kindness and firmness. I am grateful to Lord Hunt and Sir Peter Masefield for their recollections in conversation, and to the many librarians who assisted me, particularly those at the London Library, the Alpine Club, the Royal Aeronautical Society, the British Library, the Bodlean, the India Office Library, the Kensington and Chelsea Borough Library, the National Army Museum, the Rhodes House Library, the Royal Commonwealth Society, the Royal Geographical Society and the Westminster Borough Library.

I am indebted to the publishers of Virago and Eland reprints, whose imagination in this field has made my subjects so much more accessible. Dorothy Middleton and Lesley Blanche awoke my interest in women travellers when I was very young, and I should like to thank them now for their books. Mrs Penelope Currie was kind enough to give permission to reprint sections of the scrapbook of her grandmother, Mrs Agnes Huddleston.

Last but not least, I am grateful to my son, Jack Davenport, for his patience with all those adventuresses who populated our home and my conversation while I wrote this book.

CONTENTS

FOREWORD

All the women in this book embraced the opportunity to travel because it offered them independence and a redefinition of themselves outside the narrow confines of society. They rejected the submissive position of women at home, and had no particular affinity with domesticity. But if they laid the foundations of women's liberation, most of them did it unwittingly, for they were motivated by the desire for self-improvement. Although their vagaries are amusing now, they did not travel frivolously. They put a girdle round the earth by *doing*: teaching, singing, empire-building, nursing, flying, acting, hunting, dancing, climbing. A minority travelled with their husbands; few were in pursuit of a man, although some found one; most were by nature solitary, although not proof against loneliness. Many were very frail, but invalidism seems to have a mysterious link with indomitability. In any case, their upbringing had trained them to withstand hardship, for the majority came from middle-class homes that made a virtue of stoicism. Their families provided the finance necessary for their expeditions, and their nationalities gave them prestige in the countries they travelled in. With the exception of missionaries, teachers and empire-builders, on the whole they did not try to change the people they encountered.

Perhaps these three groups were the least successful travellers for they could not, like the others, simply observe curiously and accept what they found. But something all the women have in common is articulacy and inquisitiveness, which together have resulted in a formidable legacy of travel writing. In pursuit of their own goals they happily ignored convention: for all of them, 'abroad' was where they existed most fully.

The women travellers I have chosen to write about are a personal selection based mainly on affinity. Obviously I acquired new prejudices on closer acquaintance, and some of my favouritism is based on their engaging limitations. I was particularly taken with the terrible refinement of Emmeline Lott, marooned as a governess in a harem; the apparently unlimited capacity of dancer Lola Montez to lie her way out of any situation; balloonist Laetitia Sage's appetite for self-promotion; climber Annie Peck's fury at being pipped at the post by her guide at the summit of a Bolivian mountain. These foibles have made them all the more endearing.

Occasionally, though, I have become exasperated. Why did David Livingstone put his wife Mary in an ox-cart for an impossible journey every time she was pregnant, and why did she accept it? Memsahib Flora Annie Steel made me tired just reading about her polymath activities, and I felt mountaineering Fanny Bullock Workman was appropriately named, for she bullied her husband, her 'coolies' and her unfortunate female competitors. But at least these eccentricities give vivid proof of their existence. The only woman I really disliked I strongly suspect did not exist at all, or at least I suspect that her memoirs were ghosted by a man–that coyly gushing huntress, Agnes Herbert.

Some of these travellers were famous, some obscure; but because their achievements were so considerable, the real interest has been to try to see past the achievement to the personality. The vision of anthropologist Mary Kingsley prodding West African hippopotami with her umbrella, or missionary Annie Taylor solemnly making a Christmas pudding on a Tibetan mountain peak, or Mary Wortley Montagu removing her stays in a Turkish harem, or the revelation that the Hon. Misses Eden of Government House, Calcutta stank like polecats, have taken precedence over elaborately detailed accounts of their journeys. It is the quirkily revealing incident which has caught my eye, and I hope readers will be as intrigued as I have been.

It was not possible or desirable to smooth the jagged edges of these women to make them fit a neat theory. They are categorized by what they did, but even that is a crude approach because many belong in more than one chapter. I began with the idea that some categories such as missionaries or memsahibs had a particular image that my chosen examples would contradict, but in the process of research I found that the maverick missionary or memsahib was as common as the conventional one: the popular stereotype hardly existed. But of course, the interesting question is not so much what they did but why they did it.

My view of their underlying motives is necessarily subjective, yet some reasons for escapism have settled into a pattern and one can form a thesis. Others either stand isolated or remain obstinately the possession of their owner. The fascination has been to discover that though the adventuresses engaged in a lonely activity, they were not alone. What is more, to travel in their wake adds a new dimension to a shrunken world.

We are always conducting the burial service of 'real' travel and mourning its loss. First there was exploration, then there was travel, then there was tourism. These women pushed travel back towards exploration; juxtaposing their experience with ours can make us travellers as well as tourists. But perhaps it is worth remembering that the word travel comes from *travail*, with all the pain and difficulty that it implies. In 1872 Francis Galton called his book *The Art of Travel* but his subtitle makes the position clear: *Shifts and Contrivances available in wild countries*. If today we become too rigorously snobbish about tourism it is often salutary to look at Galton's advice to the brave!

> Before going to a rich but imperfectly civilised country, travellers sometimes buy jewels and bury them in their flesh to grow over them as it would over a bullet . . . the best place for burying them is in the left arm, at the spot chosen for vaccination. A traveller who was thus provided would always have a small capital to fall back on, though robbed of everything he wore.

Finally, at the risk of seeming etymologically obsessed, I confess to a grudge against words with the feminine ending -*ess*. In some cases it is implicitly diminishing: one does not expect the work of a sculptress and an authoress to be of the same calibre as that of a sculptor and an author. In other cases, -*ess* changes our expectation of the meaning: a conductress conducts a bus rather than an orchestra, and a governess governs not a country but a schoolroom. The word which has suffered the most is adventuress. To be an adventurer is a heroic business of travel and swashbuckle; to be an adventuress is to advance through society by dubious means, usually sexual. This book is an attempt to reinstate the adventuress with her original and noble meaning–an adventurer, *F*.

CLIMBERS

*A famous picture of the intrepid Le
Blond on a Norwegian peak in 1899.
Her grand aunt (in both senses of the
word grand) thought she looked like a
Red Indian, and was a social scandal.*

Until well past the turn of the century the progress of women
climbers was hampered by notions of 'respectability'. One of
the earliest female mountaineers, Frenchwoman Henriette
d'Angeville, was accused of vulgar self-promotion for her ascent
of Mont Blanc; Mrs Aubrey Le Blond, founder of the first
women's climbing club in Britain, had to fight the disapproval
of her family and social circle. Americans Fanny Bullock Workman and Annie Peck were both ardent feminists who felt their
achievements might break down barriers for their sex. Fanny
went so far as to be photographed on a Himalayan summit
brandishing the newspaper headline *Votes For Women*. Freda du
Faur, an Australian pioneer, broke new territory by shrugging
off the moralists' accusations that it was compromising to climb
alone with a male guide. Miriam Underhill and Alice Dumesme
made the first 'manless climb' together as late as 1929.

Climbing brought these women into contact with nature in
a new way, and, in the case of Freda du Faur and hymn-writer
Frances Ridley Havergal, evoked some classics of mountaineering literature. It gave them an excitement not easily available
in their middle-class lives: Gertrude Bell set the foundation for
her whole audacious career when she embraced the challenge
of the mountains. Climbing also brought the possibility of rela-
tionships outside polite society: Isabella Bird is notable not for
her mountaineering prowess, but for the freedom it gave her.

Henriette d'Angeville (1794–1871) has been unkindly described as a spinster who loved Mont Blanc because she had
nothing else to love, and was given the nickname 'La Fiancée
du Mont Blanc'. She was the first woman to climb that mountain in 1838, and her conquest of it was undeniably an obsession.
In his book *The Annals of Mont Blanc* (1898), CE Matthews describes her hunger: 'To see the fairy summit luminous at sunset
and not to be able to reach it was torture to her soul.'

Accordingly, she made meticulous preparations, took medical advice, and underwent a thorough training. She intended

to better her only female predecessor on the summit, a local woman named Maria Paradis, who had been dragged up to the top by determined guides. Giving details of her expedition to Captain Markham Sherwill, Maria had said that she was very ill on the Grand Plateau and lay down on the snow, begging the guides to drop her in a crevasse and go their own way. They insisted on hauling her up to the summit where her sense of achievement must have been limited, since she was unable to speak or breathe.

In those days no woman climbed without male guides. Henriette herself took only light provisions–her incongruous diet included lemonade, a blancmange and a few prunes–but the men in the party needed six porters to carry their food. Their appetites seem a positive liability when one reads the Lucullan list of provisions:

2 legs of mutton	1 bottle of syrop
2 ox tongues	1 cask vin ordinaire
24 fowls	12 lemons
6 large loaves	3 lbs sugar
18 bottles of St Jean	3 lbs chocolate
1 bottle of brandy	3 lbs French plums

Their party made a great impact on the local people as it departed, possibly not just because of Henriette's unusual ambition. She must have cut a strange figure, clad as she was in red flannel underclothes, woollen stockings over silk ones, Scottish tweed knickerbockers lined with flannel, a flannel blouse, a fur hat, a straw hat, a velvet mask, a veil, green specs, thick woollen gloves, a plaid and a fur-lined pelisse. By all accounts she was fearless and agile, but encumbered by all this there must have been *some* poetic licence in her observation: 'I did not walk, I flew.'

Etiquette persisted, even up an alp. During a night under canvas another climber on the same route sent across his visiting card to ask permission to call. It is a strangely formal contrast to the following day when, battling against mountain sickness, Henriette ordered her guides to drag her body to the top if she died before she reached it. But reach it she did, whereupon they lifted her up on their shoulders saying, 'Now, mademoiselle, you shall go one higher than Mont Blanc.'

Being a staunch royalist, Henriette drank a toast in champagne to the Comte de Paris and then, displaying an early grasp of public relations, dispatched a carrier pigeon to spread the news of her triumph. On her return, one of the first to embrace her was Maria Paradis.

Many women climbers initially visited the mountains for reasons of health. This was true of Frances Ridley Havergal, a frail writer of hymns who cannot be counted a great climber but whose neglected book *Swiss Letters and Alpine Poems*, written in 1882, is a charming tribute to the mountains. Here she is

Henriette d'Angeville was unkindly said to have been married to Mont Blanc and for a spinster perhaps the symbolism of mountains was unfortunate.

writing about the Col de Balme, Chamonix,

which commands one of the most sublime and perfect panoramas in the world, I should think. Here the grandest mountains in Europe are pressing close around you, a perfect abyss into the Tête Noire on one side, the perfectly graceful sweep of the valley of Chamonix on the other, aiguilles that defy the Alpine Club, glaciers between and below them linking the winter with the summer below, all one ever dreamt of alpine splendours crowded into one scene and oneself in the very centre of it, far above the waterfalls and the noisy torrents, far away from the chatter and clatter of tourists– what if one did see it at some disadvantage as to the list of peaks which ought to be visible? even with the cloud veil on her forehead, it was the most glorious revelation of Nature I have ever seen. And what was our *seat* here, up above more snow than we saw all last winter? A regular carpet of flowers, chiefly forget-me-nots, gentianellas, brilliant potentillas, violets, pansies and daisies, and many lovely flowers I did not know. The grasses too were various and pretty. What an addition to the enjoyment of the *great*, the *small* can be! And there I wrote these lines.

Sunshine and silence on the Col de Balme!
I stood above the mists, above the rush
Of all the torrents, when one marvellous hush
Filled God's great mountain temple, vast and calm,
With hallelujah light, a seen but silent psalm.

Crossed with one discord, only one. For love
Cried out and would be heard: 'If ye were here,
O friends, so far away and yet so near,
Then were the anthem perfect.' And the cry
Threaded the concords of that Alpine harmony.

Isabella Bird Bishop (1831–1904) was another of the Victorian invalids who were miraculously refreshed by the mountains. Her first trip abroad to Australia in 1872 was a drastic measure for her persistent ill-health. Australia only lowered her further, but her next stop at the Sandwich Islands (Hawaii) transformed her. She wrote to her sister Henrietta that she 'rioted most luxuriantly' in 'the congenial life of the wilds'. Her new-found energy fuelled her ascent of the slopes of the 13,650-foot Mauna Loa, the world's largest volcano.

Her next trip in 1873 was to the Rocky Mountains. Here she settled for a while in the wilderness country of Estes Park, and conducted an entirely unsuitable–though probably fundamentally respectable–relationship with a trapper named Rocky Mountain Jim, of whom her host pronounced: 'When he's sober Jim's a perfect gentleman; but when he's had liquor he's the most awful ruffian in Colorado.' Isabella's footnote to this comment was: 'But in my intercourse with him I saw more of his nobler instincts than of the darker parts of his character.'

In her letters to her sister, published in 1879, there is an irresistible account of her ascent of Long's Peak in the company of her dashing desperado. Long's Peak, 14,255 feet high, was, according to Isabella, known as the American Matterhorn. She could find no one to accompany her on an ascent until Mountain Jim took up the invitation with a small posse of undesirables. Although she wrote a stirring enough account, Isabella claimed her descriptive powers failed her, such was 'the glorious sublimity, the majestic solitude and the unspeakable awfulness and fascination of the scenes in which I spent Monday, Tuesday and Wednesday.'

One-eyed Jim was a 'shocking' figure, dressed like a gypsy and showing off his spirited Arab mare as they rode up the lower slopes. They passed through the pine forests, glimpsing purple gorges and 'the baked brown expanse' of the plains below. Made lyrical by all this beauty, Isabella was, however, chiefly moved by the spectacle of 'the notorious desperado, a red-handed man, sleeping as quietly as innocence sleeps' as they spent the night by the camp-fire in below-freezing temperatures. Together in the morning they admired the sunrise, and then began the true rigours of their climb:

Elizabeth Le Blond wore breeches beneath her skirt, and removed the latter on the higher stretches of her climb up Mont Blanc.

> Never-to-be-forgotten glories they were, burnt in upon my memory by six succeeding hours of terror. You know I have no head and no ankles, and never ought to dream of mountaineering; and had I known that the ascent was a real mountaineering feat I should not have felt the slightest ambition to perform it. As it is, I am only humiliated by my success, for 'Jim' dragged me up, like a bale of goods, by sheer force of muscle. At the 'Notch' the real business of the ascent began. Two thousand feet of solid rock towered above us, four thousand feet of broken rock shelved precipitously below; smooth granite ribs, with barely foothold, stood out here and there; melted snow, refrozen several times, presented a more serious obstacle; many of the rocks were loose, and tumbled down when touched. To me it was a time of extreme terror.

It must have been an arduous ascent–one of the young men accompanying them bled from his lungs–but Isabella modestly remarked: 'Truly terrible as it was to me, to a member of the Alpine Club it would not be a feat worth performing.'

But it was not only a considerable achievement for a stout forty-two-year-old vicar's daughter, it was a romantic pinnacle in her experience. No wonder Isabella wrote contentedly:

> A more successful ascent of the Peak was never made, and I would not now exchange my memories of its perfect beauty and extraordinary sublimity for any other experience of mountaineering in any part of the world.

Mrs Aubrey Le Blond (1861–1934), thrice-married founder of Britain's first women's climbing club, also first came to the mountains for reasons of health and with absolutely no aspirations to climb: 'In the summer of 1881 I came to Chamonix for the first time. I arrived there in bad health. As for mountaineering, I knew nothing of it and cared less.'

By 1882, however, she was displaying the same sort of obsessional symptoms as Henriette d'Angeville as she analysed her reasons for deciding to climb Col du Tacul, the one remaining untrodden col in the chain of Mont Blanc:

> It was true that it led from nothing–nowhere, but it was so strikingly and aggressively a col that someone was sure to cross it some day. Therefore if *I* made the first passage I should perform three praiseworthy actions. First, I should deprive 'somebody else' of it; secondly I should unite the glaciers of Léchaud and Géant by a passage involving a detour of about five hours from the ordinary route; and thirdly, the Aiguille du Tacul would be ascended by quite a new way.

Elizabeth Le Blond came from an extremely conventional upper middle-class background. Her mountaineering exploits met with considerable disapproval from some of her family:

> . . . I had to struggle hard for my freedom. My mother faced the music on my behalf when my grand aunt, Lady Bentinck, sent out a frantic S.O.S. 'Stop her climbing mountains. She is scandalizing all London and looks like a Red Indian.

She did not free herself from all the constraints of propriety straight away:

> An Early Victorian touch may be introduced here. Never till that moment had I put on my own boots, and I was none too sure on which foot should go which boot. It is difficult for me to realize now that for several years longer it did not occur to me that I could do without a maid, and it was not till one of the species had incessant hysteria whenever I returned late from an expedition, and another had eloped with a courier, that I gained my independence of all assistance of the sort that they did or, more often, did not render. I owe a supreme debt of gratitude to the mountains for knocking from me the shackles of conventionality.

Some shackles were never knocked away, alas. Although she climbed in trousers she always set out and returned from expeditions in a discardable skirt. On one occasion, when traversing the Zinal Rothorn, she remembered on approaching Zinal that she had left her skirt on the far side of the mountain. Unable to face the impropriety of arriving skirtless in the village, she retraced most of the day's route to fetch it.

Elizabeth Le Blond with her mask and goggles in place.

Although she was immensely respectable, it is difficult to imagine Fanny Bullock Workman (1859–1925) kow-towing to any opinions she did not share. She was as indomitable as her name suggests, and as industrious. A New Englander and a staunch feminist, she wrote floridly titled and lengthy books with her husband Dr William Hunter Workman, chronicling their travels together. They made colossal bicycle journeys 'awheel in most of the countries of Europe, in Sicily and North Africa', and then abandoned their 'trusty rovers' to climb 'afoot in the mountains of Norway, the Alps, Apennines, Pyrenees and Atlas'.

Fanny and William were middle aged when they put away their bicycles in 1898 to become pioneer Himalayan explorers. They were rather condescending travellers, particularly in their attitude to the natives who worked for them. In conversation, Lord Hunt of Everest said that he had visited the Eastern Karakoram some twenty-five years after the Workmans, but the locals were convinced that Fanny had only been gone a year, such was still the impact of her personality. About Dr Workman there was some confusion, until one of them volunteered–'Ah, yes, she had a white bearer.' Perhaps the extra duties demanded of the doctor account for the splenetic note in their recollections of yet another workforce: 'We have never met the equal of the Nagar coolies for malingering, shirking work, deserting, demanding double rations, looting grain and mutinying.' More often they adopt a loftily knowledgeable tone, delivering this homily of experts to the uninformed, for instance in *Ice-bound Heights of the Mustagh* (1908):

> Certain philanthropically disposed persons, having little or no knowledge of coolies under the conditions here considered, talk of the efficacy of kind treatment–which means coddling and making companions of them–in inducing them to remain faithful to their agreements. We do not wish to be understood as advocating harsh treatment of coolies or anyone else. Far from it. But our experience leads us to agree with those who, having had much to do with coolies under varying conditions, regard this idea as mere sentimental nonsense.
>
> It has been said to us time and again by those long in the Indian service, and we have had every reason to believe it to be in general true, that the coolie understands only the application of superior force as an incentive to fulfil his obligations. Gratitude he does not know. Kindness he does not appreciate nor reciprocate, and ordinary motives of personal advantage, as understood by Europeans, do not always appeal to him. He is an Asiatic, unswayed by those principles which regulate the conduct of conscientious Europeans. It is not necessary to treat him harshly, but he must be handled with firmness. Either you must master him or he will master you. He knows no middle ground. The more kindness you bestow on him, the more he will leave you in the lurch, and

steal from you if he can. The principle of equal privilege for all cannot safely be extended to him, as has been abundantly shown during the past few years by the evil effects of the doubtless well-meant efforts to improve his lot, not only in Kashmir, but also in India, by relaxing the conditions under which he serves the public. The more these have been relaxed the more unreliable has he become, and the less efficient his service. Not being able to comprehend the value of privilege, he has prostituted it to base ends, to the detriment of the position of the Anglo-Indian, as is apparent to those conversant with the trend of Indian affairs during the last ten years. The coolie has been unduly elevated, the public interest has suffered.

Fanny Bullock Workman, the intrepid New Englander, seen here in a crevasse, wrote. '. . . we had breathed the atmosphere of that great mountain-world, had drunk of the swirling waters of its glaciers, and feasted our eyes on the comparable beauty and majesty of its towering peaks, and, as time passed on, its charms asserted their power anew and called to us with irresistable siren strains to return once again to those regions the grandeur of which satisfies so fully the sense of the beautiful and sublime.'

Fanny was blessed with an iron constitution. Aged forty in 1899, she created the altitude record for women when she climbed the 21,000-foot Mount Gunge. This is her own rather throw-away account of her stamina, taken from her first mountaineering book *In the Ice World of the Himalaya* (1900). It is intended as an encouragement to her sex, but may not have had precisely that effect:

For the benefit of women, who may not yet have ascended to altitudes above 16,000 feet but are thinking of attempting to do so, I will here give my experiences for what they are worth.

I began the march from Srinagar to Balristan within four weeks of the completion of a rather exhausting cycle trip in tropical Java, where . . . I had been doing little walking, with the exception of climbing a few Javan volcanoes, which was not invigorating exercise even at heights of 11,000 and 12,000 feet. Two weeks and a half after leaving Batavia were spent in lying around inactive on the decks of steamers, on the train crossing the heated plains of India, in a temperature of 104° to 107° Fahr. for seventy-two hours at Rawal Pindi, and in a *tonga* from that place to Srinagar. It will thus be seen that, in starting out, I was in no especial training for mountain work.

I am not a light weight and am a slow climber. Still my powers of endurance on long days of climbing, and in weeks of continued cycle touring, have, for a number of years, been good. I had been told by people in England and also in India, that I should not be able to cycle more than one cold weather in the plains, and certainly should not be fit for much in the mountains after a long season of exposure to the sun at lower altitudes. As a matter of fact, my hardest and highest mountain work was accomplished after two seasons, of six months each, cycling in Ceylon, India, and Java.

On all their expeditions Fanny and William were well organized and practical; they were brave and tenacious; they took excellent and valuable photographs. There was a time when it was fashionable to suggest that the Watermans exaggerated the heights they achieved. However, they were fastidious about detail and accuracy, as this daunting summary of a chapter of *Ice-bound Heights of the Mustagh* suggests:

Chapter XV
Importance of Altitude–Measurements–Mercurial Barometer–Hypsometer, Uses and Limitations–Aneroid–Liable to Index–Errors–Useful when properly Checked–Experiments with Watkin Aneroids–Shut-off Feature of Questionable Value–Different Aneroids develop Different Errors

In 1906 Fanny achieved an undisputed new record with her conquest of the 23,000-foot Pinnacle Peak in Kashmir. Climbers often used stimulants, and Fanny pays grudging tribute to a drug that kept up her energy after three sleepless days and nights:

Perhaps the use of granular kola . . . may have had a tonic effect. This in proper doses seems to be a good pick-me-up in cases of fatigue, or where a continued physical strain must be undergone. If, however, taken in too large quantity, it produces giddiness and a feeling of lassitude, like other substances containing alkaloids.

A deck-board photograph of Miss Peck with her two Swiss guides. The bearded gentleman lurking behind is named in the contemporary caption merely as 'scientist'.

When another woman challenged this hard-won altitude record, Fanny was outraged. Her fellow-American Annie Peck (1850–1935) claimed to have achieved 24,000 feet on Mount Huascaran in Peru in 1908. Fanny records her doubts with some asperity in *The Call of the Snowy Hispar on the Higher Himalayas*: 'These contentions being based, confessedly on eye-estimates only . . . were naturally regarded with incredulity by geographers, engineers and mountaineers.'

At her own expense, Fanny sent a topographical expedition to Peru to measure the offending peak. The results triumphantly demolished poor Miss Peck's claim:

> And they show that the altitude of the lower summit of Huascaran, claimed to have been ascended by Miss Peck, is some 1,500 feet lower than the highest altitude attained by Mrs Bullock Workman.

Despite this slur on her veracity, it is much easier to like Annie Peck, who in contrast to the immensely rich Workmans had to struggle and pinch to mount every expedition, and probably could not afford the topographical instruments necessary for accuracy. Her reasons for climbing varied at different times in her life, as she explains in her autobiographical book *High Mountain Climbing in Peru and Bolivia*. Her first sight of the Matterhorn is an echo of Henriette d'Angeville's reaction to Mont Blanc:

'[I] . . . felt that I should never be happy until I, too, should scale those frowning walls which have beckoned so many upwards, a few to their own destruction.'

She found the exercise on smaller climbs 'delightful and invigorating', enjoying the 'exhilarating atmosphere', 'the charm of the ever varying vista' and 'the stillness and solitude'. Then she became seized with the idea of exploration 'to attain some height where no *man* [her italics] had previously stood'. She wanted to make a contribution to science by meteorological and geological observation. If Fanny Workman had not been busy scrapping about altitude records, she would undoubtedly have agreed with Annie Peck that 'any great achievement in any line of endeavour would be of advantage to my sex'. Her interest aroused by the unconquered peaks in South America, Annie hoped her exploits might help to open up the relationship between the USA and South America. She wanted to promote travel and commercial ventures, such as the construction of the Pan American Railway, feeling that anything which deepened the understanding of unfamiliar countries was an even more important concept than adding to scientific knowledge.

These edifying sentiments needed funding to get off the ground, but Annie Peck discovered that most of her sympathizers were distinctly impecunious. She needed $5,000 and when various newspapers and magazines refused to sponsor her she offered individual subscriptions of $100, but there were very few takers. Advertisers of food, chocolate, shoes and soap did not avail themselves of the opportunity either. Miss Peck ruefully remarked, 'What a chance was lost for saying, "Soapine did it!"'

Her financial difficulties were never resolved on the South American trip–'The disheartening struggle continued to the last moment preceding the final triumph.' As a result, she set out on her climbs 'so meagerly financed and equipped as to be compelled to serve as porter, cook, photographer, scientific man and general boss all at the same time'. Her poverty and the exigencies of fund-raising meant that she had no proper physical training for any expedition:

> I heartily recommend such a course . . . but I have had no opportunity. On my four trips to South America I have gone on board ship at New York a perfect wreck; each time . . . a little worse than before, having taken practically no exercise between voyages.

Fifteen thousand feet up Illampu in Bolivia, she observed: 'Unfortunately it is three years since I have done any climbing or had any training of any sort.' It was just as well that she held the theory '. . . sometimes mountain climbers, like poets, may be born not made.' Her equipment was of necessity fairly rudimentary: no oxygen, a barometer and a hypsometer. Her opinions on suitable mountaineering attire differed radically

Annie Peck and her party on the hotel patio as they left for a climb in Peru.

from those of the socially conscious Mrs Le Blond. She wore an Eskimo suit for climbing.

> A skirt . . . however short and light, anything depending from the waist or shoulders, is some hindrance to movement and of noticeable weight. I had not an ounce of strength to spare for superfluities, neither do I consider that an abbreviated skirt would add to the gracefulness of my appearance or that if it did, that this, upon the mountain, would be of the slightest consequence.

Her provisions were elementary: soups, tea, chocolate, grapenuts, canned meat, raisins and sugar. For stamina, they chewed coca leaves: 'for our own use as well as for the Indians'. They also carried four quarts of cheap alcohol; it is rather startling to discover that three of these were for the Indians and one *of better quality* was to light the kerosene stove.

The ascent of Illampu was a failure, perhaps not entirely surprisingly in view of the poor equipment and her lack of fitness. Both contributed to her difficulties when she was crossing a crevasse and trying to get a firm hold above with her ice axe: 'But the axe dull and my muscle unequal to the task.' The lack of experience in her team was a grave handicap—

> Turning then for the first time to summon to my aid the cholo [mestizo] who when I set out had been tied on the other end of the rope, I saw to my horror and disgust the rope trailing idly on the snow, the two men where I had left them. On a steep and dangerous slope, on the very brink of a crevasse into which a careless step would have plunged me, and no-one on the rope! A little less caution and I should be in the bottom of that crevasse now!

Her escort on that occasion, Mr Victor Sintich, had a little experience of snow-climbing in Bolivia, but he had never made a complete ascent of Illampu and now urged her to abandon the attempt. 'Oh, how I longed for a man with enough pluck and determination to stand by me to the finish.'

Her five attempts on Mount Huascarán in Peru were dogged by similar problems. She had to instruct the Indians in everything, including the use of ropes. It was impossible to succeed without proper assistants. Annie Peck was commendably longsuffering about the general ineptitude. When one of her Indians took off his pack (believing he would look smarter without it in a photograph) and promptly lost it down a crevasse, she merely comments: 'I especially lamented the loss of a fine pair of field-glasses.' On another of her attempts her companion, the anonymous E–, who had a previous history of insanity, apparently harboured a desire to kill her. In the circumstances her reaction is a laconic one: 'While regretting that my attempts on Huascarán had turned out so badly, I congratulated myself on getting back alive and resolved never again to go climbing with one who has been really mad.'

After all these disasters she decided, reasonably enough, that experienced Swiss guides were what she needed for her fifth attempt. This in itself was not without problems.

> One of the chief difficulties in a woman's undertaking an expedition of this nature is that every man believes he knows better what should be done than she. The Indians are not aggressive and, unless through indolence or fear, are likely to do as they are bidden; though even these, in descending below the snow, urged their own notions of the proper route, in opposition to my experience. The crazy man, E–, in 1906, was confident that two days on the snow supplied him with complete and superior knowledge, while my companions in Bolivia, both scientific and otherwise, alike believed that they could give me points in all matters, whatever my experience and their lack. It is not strange, therefore, that in common with my previous assistants, the Swiss guides who had come over for this purpose and were well skilled in their calling should conclude that my three abortive efforts on this side of the mountain counted for nothing in comparison with their own judgement. When I suggested a certain line of ascent, a certain place found best for the first camp, they said, especially Rudolf, the elder, 'Oh, yes! but then glaciers change every season, as well as from day to day. Better this ridge!' As the matter was not vital I did not insist, with the result that we encamped at last too far south, at a higher point than was desirable, where no brush could be gathered for fire, and whence we were obliged next day to make a tiresome and unnecessary traverse.

The relationship with Rudolf was not a success. Even in retrospect she was furious at his careless loss of her fur mittens, leaving her only with inadequate wool ones: 'Twitching off my mittens I found that the hand was nearly black. Rubbing it vigorously with snow, I soon had it aching badly which signified its restoration.' Admittedly he got her to the summit, but even there he had the temerity to pip her to the post:

> I *was* enraged. I had told them, long before, that as it was my expedition I should like, as is customary, to be the first one to place my foot at the top, even though I reached it through their instrumentality. It would not lessen their honour and I was paying the bills.

There was a rough justice in the sequel to these events, for frostbite acquired on the descent brought an end to Rudolf's mountaineering career. His left hand, a finger on his right, and half a foot had to be amputated. Displaying a barely acceptable amount of sympathy, Mrs Peck implied that he was carelessly equipped for the cold. It certainly accounts for the fact that he did not lend her his own mittens.

In contrast, Freda du Faur, the Australian mountaineer, owed her remarkable career to the skilful teaching of her guide Peter Graham, then in the prime of his climbing life. She was his aptest pupil and readily absorbed his experienced views. As a young woman in 1906, mere tourist curiosity took her to Mount Cook in New Zealand, as she describes in her book *The Conquest of Mount Cook*, which must surely be a classic of mountaineering literature:

> I had no thought of climbing, I was merely filled with curiosity to see something that was quite outside my experience, so at the end of December I set out.
>
> People who live amongst the mountains all their lives, who have watched them at sunrise and sunset, in midday heat or moonlight glow, love them, I believe, as they love the sun and flowers, and take them as much for granted. They have no conception how the first sight of them strikes to the very heart-strings of that less fortunate individual, the hill-lover who lives in a mountainless country. From the moment my eyes rested on the snow-clad alps I worshipped their beauty and was filled with a passionate longing to touch those shining snows, to climb to their heights of silence and solitude, and feel myself one with the mighty forces around me. The great peaks towering into the sky before me touched a chord that all the wonders of my own land had never set vibrating, and filled a blank of whose very existence I had been unconscious. Many people realize the grandeur and beauty of the mountains, who are quite content to admire them from a distance, if strenuous physical exertion is the price they must pay for a nearer acquaintance. My chief desire as I gazed at them was to reach the snow and bury my hands in its wonderful whiteness, and dig and dig till my snow-starved Australian soul was satisfied that all this wonder of white was real and would not vanish at the touch.

One scramble on the Sealy range convinced her 'that earth held no greater joy than to be a mountaineer'. From the beginning she fought the battle for emancipation in all matters mountaineering. She found that she was 'up against all the cherished conventions of the middle-aged who assured me in all seriousness that if I went out alone with a guide I would lose my reputation'. She pandered to the proprieties by taking a second guide on the Sealy climb, but as her fame grew she became free to do as she pleased and simply ignored the carpings of the self-appointed moralists.

It was two years before she was able to take a holiday again. She returned to renew her pupil relationship with Peter Graham, the chief guide at the Hermitage:

This cover of the Ladies' Alpine Club journal was engraved by Una Cameron, herself a notable climber.

LADIES' ALPINE CLUB

1925

Freda du Faur, the Australian, wore conventional dress but fought the battle for emancipation in all matters of mountaineering.

From various causes my holiday was limited to a fortnight, but short though it was it was long enough to settle the question of my capabilities. I was fortunate in always going out with parties that were under the charge of the chief guide, and which usually included no other woman. Very soon Graham realized that I was always the most enthusiastic, and often the fittest of the party at the end of the day, so he began to watch me carefully. One day three of us climbed with him to a pass immediately beneath the third summit of Mount Cook; it was the highest point to which I had ascended. As I stood on the summit I felt that my question was answered. I could do what I would. Silently I gazed at the thin, jagged ridge in front of me leading up to Mount Cook. Then and there I decided I would be a real mountaineer, and some day be the first woman to climb Mount Cook.

She was not only the first woman to climb Mt Cook, but in 1913 she did so in record time: 'I gained the summit . . . feeling very little, very lonely and much inclined to cry.'

The First World War put an end to Freda du Faur's climbing career. She died in her native Australia in 1935 and is best remembered not only for her skills as a mountaineer, but for her happy philosophy of the mountains:

As the car rushed away across the plains a mist for a moment blotted out the towering mountains, the blue sky, and the brown faces of my comrade guides, with a lump in my throat I waved a last farewell. Life is opening out, I may see many lands and make many friends, but as long as it shall last I will carry with me an imperishable memory of that happy home among the mountains, memories of good friends and true, of brave deeds quietly done–days of exultation and triumph, days of sorrow and failure.

Miriam Underhill, who has been described as the best woman climber America ever produced, had her first glimpse of the Alps as a child in the year that Freda du Faur stopped climbing. She inherited the feminist mantle of her predecessors, for in 1929 she was the first woman ever to do a 'manless climb'. She resented the notion that her climbing was 'only following' a leader, whether he were guide or amateur, and saw no reason why a woman should be incapable of leading a climb, despite adverse male reaction to her claim. Her choice was the Grépon, one of the finest rock-climbs in the Alps, and one which not all the Chamonix guides were licensed to do. Accordingly, she set out with Alice Dumesme to achieve the first manless traverse of the Grépon. There was considerable pressure from below: 'The bergschrund [crevasse across the head of a glacier] really did give us quite a lot of trouble, but we couldn't waste much time on it with that large and rapidly growing audience below.'

Even though they achieved their object there was male disparagement to face. In her autobiography *Give Me The Hills*, Miriam Underhill records a man's comment on the evening of their descent:

> The Grépon has disappeared . . . as a climb it no longer exists. Now that it has been done by two women alone, no self-respecting man can undertake it. A pity, too, because it used to be a very good climb.

The true test, as far as Miriam and Alice were concerned, would be a manless ascent of the Matterhorn. That elusive mountain took years rather than weeks to conquer, and it was not until 1932 that they were successful. There was a reception in Chamonix in their honour–flowers, a band, ovations–but instead Miriam went over to the Eastern Alps to join some friends, including Robert Underhill who was to become her husband: 'After that for nineteen years my constant companion on every climb was Robert Underhill. Manless climbing is fun for a while, but this other arrangement is better!'

Another cover from the Ladies' Alpine Club journal.

Women climbers were a source of inspiration to each other, and it is fascinating to discover that Miriam Underhill decided to repeat some of the climbs of Gertrude Bell (1868–1926), whom she described as 'that extraordinary woman . . . as outstanding in mountaineering as in the fields of exploration, archaeology and diplomacy'. Gertrude Bell's own books and her excellent biography by HVF Winstone concentrate mainly on what she described as her 'true call': her life in the Middle East. We are more accustomed to reading of her desert exploits; it is not so widely known that between 1901 and 1904 she was an acclaimed climber in the Swiss Alps. Her letters from Switzerland to her family are an irresistible blend of boasting, self-depreciation and girlish high spirits. Here she describes climbing the Schreckhorn in Grindlewald in 1901:

> It's a capital bit of rock climbing, a razor edge going quite steep down, snow on one side and rock on the other, not quite solid so that you have to take the greatest care.

Her party had left provisions and wood in a hut for their return, but on their descent they found three Frenchmen burning the wood and making the tea.

> I said politely that I was delighted to entertain them, but that I hoped they would let us have some of the tea, since it was really ours. They looked rather black but made no apologies, nor did they thank me and I went away to change my things outside. When I came back they had gone but they left the following entry in the visitors' book: 'Nous sommes montés au refuge sans guides. Vue splendide! mais quelle faim! Heureusement nous avons trouvé du thé.' I completed the entry by adding 'N.B. It was my tea!' and signing my name . . .

Miss Meta Brevoot, the American climber is famous on two counts. First, she climbed in the Alps when this was mainly a male activity, accompanied by her dog, Tschingel. Second, she introduced her nephew to climbing and he in turn became a famous Alpine mountaineer– W A B Coolidge.

Very soon Gertrude's skills were rivalling those of the experienced guides.

Well, here we were on an awfully steep place under the overhanging place. Ulrich tried it on Heinrich's shoulder and could not reach any hold. I then clambered up on to Heinrich, Ulrich stood on me and fingered up the rock as high as he could. It wasn't high enough. I lifted myself still a little higher–always with Ulrich on me, mind!–and he began to raise himself by his hands. As his foot left my shoulder I put up a hand, straightened out my arm and made a ledge for him. He called out, 'I don't feel at all safe; if you move we are all killed.' I said, 'All right, I can stand here for a week,' and up he went by my shoulder and my hand. It was just high enough. Once up, he got into a fine safe place and it was now my turn. I was on Heinrich's shoulder still with one foot and with one on the rock. Ulrich could not help me because he hadn't got my rope–I had been the last on the rope, you see, and I was going up second, so that all I had was the rope between the two guides to hold on to. It was pretty hard work, but I got up. Now we had to get Heinrich up. He had a rope round his waist and my rope to hold, but no shoulder, but he could not manage it. The fact was, I think, that he lost his nerve, anyhow, he declared that he could not get up, not with 50 ropes, and there was

29

Gertrude Bell, best-known as a Middle East expert, was also an outstanding mountaineer in the Alps, and an exceptionally brave woman.

A cartoon of Gertrude Bell at an Oriental party in her later Middle East days.

From Trebizond to Tripolis
She rolls the Pashas flat
And tells them what to think of this
And what to think of that

nothing to do but to leave him. He unroped himself from the big rope and we let down the thin rope to him, with which he tied himself, while we fastened our end firmly on to a rock. There we left him like a second Prometheus–fortunately there were no vultures about! So Ulrich and I went on alone and got as far as the top of the first great slab.

Gertrude's father later expanded on this, enhancing his daughter's courageous reputation still further:

I must add as a footnote to this letter that when Gertrude came home to us and related the thrilling ascent, still more exciting naturally in the telling, she told us that after it was over Ulrich had said to her, 'If, when I was standing on your shoulders and asked you if you felt safe, you had said you did not, I should have fallen and we should all have gone over.' And Gertrude replied to him, 'I thought I was falling when I spoke.'

On her departure from her first season's serious climbing, Gertrude wrote home an engagingly schoolgirlish summary of her very considerable achievements:

Rosenlaui 1901
I am very sorry to leave this nice place.
What do you think is our fortnight's bag?
Two old peaks.
Seven new peaks–one of them first class and four others very good.
One new saddle, also first class.
The traverse of the Engelhorn, also new and first class.
That's not bad going, is it!

Miriam Underhill repeated several of Gertrude Bell's climbs, but the most challenging was the north-east face of the Finsteraarhorn. Gertrude was thwarted two-thirds of the way up by bad weather conditions. Her descent was a horror story of thunderstorms, snowstorms, nights spent tied to the rocks or huddled together in pouring rain on the glacier. On the whole, Gertrude underplays the difficulties in her account, presenting it rather as a ripping yarn, but even she confesses: 'seriously, now that I am comfortably indoors, I do rather wonder that we ever got down the Finsteraarhorn and that we were not frozen at the bottom of it.' She rallies enough to make a joke about frostbite–'I don't expect I shall be toeless.'

Miriam Underhill's autobiographical recollection of the climb is altogether bleaker and more frightening: 'Even today that climb remains a very unpleasant memory.' As in Gertrude's attempt, conditions were very bad: severe ice and the additional hazard of breaking and falling rock. Miriam was hit by a fall of stones:

But although the physical damage was slight, this was the first in a long series of events which that day nearly wore through my rather fragile courage. I have always been afraid of objective dangers (those arising from external circumstances) and in particular of falling stones.

There is even an uncanny reminder of Gertrude's letter of 1901, when she saved her guide:

> Although I couldn't see Fritz, I knew—physically, perhaps!—that he was going to fall off a split second before he did so, and had just time to take a quick turn of his rope around my right hand. Otherwise I am sure I should not have been able to hold it. At the same time I took a turn of the rope above my head around my left hand. This was not strictly necessary because of course the rope was tied to my waist anyway, but it prevented a jerk where the rope went around my body, and perhaps gave a certain amount of spring to the whole system. Fritz took a really stupendous fall. Since I was not much above him, and far out to the side, he executed a long-radius pendulum, fast and far, before finally coming to rest on the perpendicular ice slope below our chimney, out of sight of both of us. The force of his fall pulled me out away from the wall, and his additional weight on the rope so stretched the section from Adolf to me that when the system finally settled into equilibrium, although my toes were still on their small holds, my body was nearly horizontal. Both my hands, however, were still holding their ropes.

Few could have carried their feminism to such peaks as Fanny Bullock Workman who placed her 'Votes for Women' placard on a summit in the Karakorum. She was a staunch defender of her sex, saying, 'It is to be hoped that light may fall upon the souls of men that they may realise the great injustice practised upon the weaker sex.'

These women, and the many other accomplished mountaineers not mentioned here, did not climb mountains 'because they are there', the usual justification for what is to most people an incomprehensible obsession, but to help define themselves to themselves. Each would have been narrower without the experience. All of them contributed something to sexual equality, for climbing is more than a question of endurance, as Miriam Underhill observed during her climbs in the Dolomites:

> In common with many women, I felt that these Dolomites were made just to suit me, with their small but excellent toe- and finger-holds, and pitches where a delicate sense of balance was the key rather than brute force. While it helps of course to have tough muscles, the prize-fighter would not necessarily make a fine Dolomite climber. But the ballet-dancer might.

CHAPTER 2

ACTRESSES, DIVAS AND DANCERS

Lola Montez had a markedly sadistic vein and, when annoyed, was not above laying about her with a dog-whip which 'she always carried', says a biographer, surely employing hyperbole. She had a pet bulldog too. Here, the cartoonist has used these elements to satirize the party she chose to act as her bodyguard, known as Alemannia, when she lived under the protection of Ludwig of Bavaria. Her relations with the latter, she insisted, were purely platonic.

Tour de force or forced to tour? Internationally famous stage performers, who caused a sensation in far-flung outposts as well as capital cities, were a brief phenomenon made possible by an audience eager to worship. They were generally even more exalted abroad than at home. As Henry Knepler writes in *The Gilded Stage*: 'They came like fairy princesses from afar . . . after long and perilous voyages on board ship to bestow–in person–on Lima, Peru or Melbourne, Australia or Milwaukee, Wisconsin, membership in the inner circle of great world culture.' But there are no more travelling princesses of the theatre for the advent of film has distributed stars around the globe.

The early peripatetic performers displayed their talents abroad for a variety of reasons. It needed a high degree of motivation to endure back-breaking touring schedules. The fascinating Spanish dancer Lola Montez moved ever onwards because of failure and scandal; the 'Swedish Nightingale', Jenny Lind (who had just cancelled her marriage plans), travelled as an antidote to sadness and to consolidate her success at home; the French actress Elise Rachel's priorities were straightforwardly basic: 'What a trip! What fatigue!! But what loot!!!'

Sarah Bernhardt quarrelled with her management, alienated her public in France and defiantly took the rest of the world by storm; Marie Lloyd, the great music hall star, travelled to minimize the snub of exclusion from a Royal Command Performance in London. The prima ballerina Anna Pavlova possessed more cultural zeal than any of these: she was inspired by the travels of the nineteenth-century ballerina Taglioni with the idea of taking her art to as many places as possible. It must be admitted that her repertoire was expressly designed to display *her* talent to the best advantage, rather than that of her company. (A member of that company alive today complains that she fed them all hot chocolate to make them fat and herself more ethereal by comparison!) Isadora Duncan spread her own gospel of the dance, but her picaresque progress on tour was less reminiscent of Pavlova than of Montez.

It is hard to pinpoint a time in the life of Lola Montez (1818–1861) when she was not the focus of some sort of attention. She is one of the very few adventuresses in this book of whom the corrupted sexual sense of the word is completely descriptive. She stands apart from the international stars who succeeded her because, unlike them, she was never a great artist. She was, however, a consummate *succès de scandale*. She supplies many exotic variations on her own story in her notoriously unreliable memoirs, but it seems reasonably certain that she was born Marie Dolores Gilbert in Limerick in 1818. Aged four, she travelled with her mother and father to India when he joined his regiment at Dinapore. He died of cholera soon after, whereupon his ravishing widow promptly married his best friend, Captain Craigie. In a year or two Craigie rose to the rank of colonel, his new wife becoming an Anglo-Indian station queen and Lola receiving her first taste of adulation as the exquisite little goddess of a regiment. Like all Anglo-Indian children she was sent 'home' for her education, which ranged from Craigie's Calvinist relations (who spoilt her) to a Parisian finishing school.

In 1837 she returned from France to rejoin her mother in Bath, where a marriage had been arranged for her to a rich, elderly Supreme Court Judge from Calcutta. However, also in Bath was a good-looking young officer, Lieutenant Thomas James. Lola eloped. Back in India as a young bride and distinctly untypical memsahib, she became the belle of Calcutta and Simla. Sharp-eyed Emily Eden, sister of the Governor-General, wrote about Lola with some prescience:

> Very pretty and a good little thing apparently, but they are poor, and she is young and lively, and if she falls into bad hands she would soon laugh herself into foolish scrapes. At present the husband and wife are very fond of each other, but a girl who marries at fifteen hardly knows what she likes.

As a matter of fact, it was James who had not known what he liked, for he soon eloped with another, and Lola was forced to return to her mother and stepfather. A social embarrassment, she was packed off to relatives in England. But Lola committed adultery on the journey home with Captain Lennox, ADC to the Governor of Madras, and once in London proceeded to move in with him. It was scandalous behaviour for the period and meant a total loss of Lola's 'reputation'. Lieutenant James initiated divorce proceedings against her–which he never completed–and Lola's mother indicated her disapproval by going into heavy mourning. Captain Lennox then abandoned the relationship, but rather than slipping easily into the life of a courtesan (for she was besieged with offers), Lola began to study Spanish dancing.

After four months' training she was hired by Benjamin

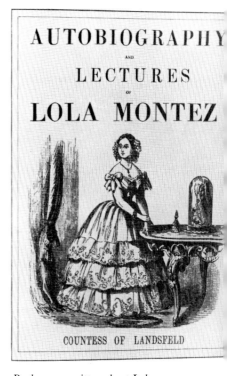

AUTOBIOGRAPHY
AND
LECTURES
OF
LOLA MONTEZ

COUNTESS OF LANDSFELD

Books were written about Lola Montez in her lifetime, as they still are today, and she also published her own views in Arts of Beauty.

Lumley, impresario of Her Majesty's Theatre and billed as: 'Donna Lola Montez, *première danseuse* from the Teatro Real, Madrid.'

Men ruined the dancing career of Lola Montez and she in turn ruined men. The pattern began at that first performance, which was sabotaged by a spurned suitor, Lord Ranelagh. Hissing her from the boxes with his cronies, he shouted out that she was not Lola Montez but 'Betsy James, an Irish girl'. The audience had liked her, the notices were good, but Ranelagh continued to spread rumours that she was an impostor with a discreditable past. Lola's contract was terminated.

It was never her style to ignore criticism, and with commendable spirit (but extraordinary amnesia about her antecedents), she wrote a letter to all the papers on 13 June 1843:

> I am a native of Seville . . . until the 14th of April when I landed in England I have never set foot in this country and I never saw London before in my life.

Her failure drove her to the Continent, and according to her memoirs she was a great success in Dresden and Berlin before going on to Warsaw. Another version is that she could find no employment and was reduced to pawning her clothes and singing in the street, until she was escorted to Warsaw by a German who suggested she try for an engagement at the Opera there. She was a success, not only with the public but with Franz Liszt who deserted his mistress and his wife for a brief and passionate liaison with her. But as in London, her triumph as a dancer was spoiled by a rejected suitor. Prince Paskievitch, the Russian Viceroy and brutal oppressor of the Poles, ruined her performance for three nights with a claque hired to hiss her. By her own account, she rushed to the footlights to explain to the rest of the house, exposing the Prince's shoddy tactics. The audience not only cheered her, but escorted her home to her lodgings. Paskievitch tried to have her expelled from Poland and she would have been imprisoned but for the intervention of the French Consul (presumably enslaved) who claimed she was a French subject.

By 1844 she was in Paris, appearing once only at the Opéra. It was not a success, nor was her only other engagement at the Porte Martin. On both occasions she told the audience what she thought of them. But she left Paris richer than she arrived, the possessor of a legacy. Needless to say, it was not a moral tale. Her lover Dujarier, literary editor of *La Presse*, had fought a duel with the dramatic critic of *Le Globe* and been killed. The beneficiary Lola was called as a witness. She declared she was a better shot than poor Dujarier and would have fought the dramatic critic herself. It seems entirely probable.

With her legacy she went fortune-hunting in Germany. 'The moment I get a nice round sum I am going to try to hook a prince,' she had said. But the only one who asked her to stay also asked her to leave when she walked over his flower-beds. She moved on to the Court Theatre, Munich, where the director was not sufficiently impressed to hire her. With her other talent she enlisted the support of a royal ADC, and through him she obtained an introduction to King Ludwig I of Bavaria. Sixty years old, a cultured man, he received her and was lost: 'I am bewitched.'

As a result of her witchcraft, the director of the Court Theatre was overruled and Lola appeared at a Royal Command Performance. With the benefit of royal approval she had a triumph. There were, to be sure, some hisses, and rumours that she was both a spy and a disreputable character, but Ludwig was further enchanted and ordered a second performance. This time the claque carried out their orders to give Lola an ovation.

From then on Lola's career took an extraordinary and dramatic sidestep into affairs of state. Ludwig brought her to Court–'Gentlemen, I present to you my best friend'–and paid her private and public homage. Privately, he wrote her poetry and had her portrait painted, spending hours in silent contemplation of it. He took Spanish lessons from her, though she cannot have been much help. The relationship between the sixty-year-old king and the twenty-nine-year-old beauty was the butt of the newspapers. Publicly, Ludwig protected her position in every way he could. He banished the chief of police for criticizing her, he gave her Bavarian nationality, estates, an income and a title. The new Countess of Lansfield proved herself an able politician, and under her guidance Ludwig's notoriously reactionary policies became perceptibly more liberal. 'I will not give up Lola. I never will give her up. My kingdom for Lola.'

Living like a queen, consulted over matters of state, when Lola fell from power she took the King with her. University students were demonstrating against her outside her house, and since she was never slow to remonstrate with an unsympathetic audience, she came out to face them. They yelled insults: she lost her temper. 'I shall have the University closed.' She had to seek sanctuary from the crowd in a church, and was finally rescued by troops. Ludwig supported her by closing the University, but the town of Munich rebelled. It was the end of the reign of Lola. Ludwig capitulated to the opinion of his people, she was ordered to leave Bavaria, and her palace was looted. Typically, she ignored the banishment and crept back disguised as a boy. But Ludwig's betrayal of her was complete: persuaded that her influence over him was indeed witchcraft, he sent her to an exorcist. Put on a starvation diet, mesmerized and given asses' milk, Lola soon escaped to Switzerland.

Back in London her theatrical career flickered fitfully into life again; she played an engagement at Covent Garden billed as 'Lola Montez: *ou la Comtesse pour une heure*'. Then she retired into private life on her Bavarian money. But since her dancing had always been the sideshow to the main event of her private life, it was not long before she was again the focus of delighted

In the 'Gallery of Beauties' in Munich is this portrait of Lola Montez, painted at the command of the sixty-year-old King Ludwig I of Bavaria who asserted, 'I am bewitched' and called her his 'best and dearest friend'. He created her Comtesse de Lanasfeld, perhaps knowing that she hailed from Limerick, although her name was hardly Irish and her soubriquet was 'The Spanish Dancer'.

Jenny Lind, the Swedish Nightingale, travelled as an antidote to the sadness of a broken engagement of marriage. Eventually, she married her accompanist and settled down in England, where she became Professor of Singing at the Royal College of Music.

gossip. In 1849 she married a young guardsman named George Trafford Heald, convinced that she was already divorced. But Thomas James was still alive in India, and Lola was arrested on a charge of bigamy. Disraeli wrote with relish:

> The Lola Montez marriage makes a sensation . . . She quite convinced him previously she was not Mrs James; and as for the King of Bavaria, who, by the by, allows her £1,500 a year and to whom she writes every day–that was only a *malheureuse* passion.

The marriage failed (Heald was subsequently drowned while bathing in the Tagus) and Lola tried her luck again on stage in America in 1851, but with no success. Despite the bigamy charge she married again–to the editor of the *San Francisco Whig*. She left him speedily for a German doctor named Adler, who was killed out shooting. Indefatigably on she went, this time to Australia, where she made a tour of the principal towns. She had a fair success, but at Ballarat felt compelled to horsewhip a local editor for his review of her performance.

In 1857 Lola returned to America for the last four years of her life. She gave autobiographical lectures (with imaginative embellishments), and in 1858 published *Arts of Beauty*, which includes a chapter on *A Beautiful Bosom* in which she enquires, 'Why should not a woman be suitably instructed in the right management of such extraordinary charms?' By 1860 she was helping her own sex in a less frivolous way by visiting outcast women in the Magdalen Asylum. The onset of piety was not unconnected with the fact she felt her end was near, and in 1861, stricken with paralysis, she died, aged forty-three, 'sincerely penitent'. Her epitaph might be taken from her own lecture on *Heroines in History*: 'The experience of the world has pretty well proved that a man's judgement is pretty easily controlled when his heart is once persuaded.'

Jenny Lind (1820–1887) was a monument of respectability in her touring days and in his memoir of her, Canon Scott Holland expressed horror at the mere possibility of her encountering Lola Montez as a member of her audience:

> The time fixed for this visit to Munich was, in one respect, most unpropitious; and, for a young artist, unsupported by powerful moral protection, the visit itself might well have proved extremely unpleasant. It was impossible to sing at Court, for the reigning spirit in the household of King Ludwig I was the notorious Lola Montez, who was then at the climax of her ill-gotten power. To have been brought into contact with such a person would have been intolerable. An invitation to Court would have rendered such contact inevitable.

The genius at promotion of the day was Barnum, who was obsessed with bringing Jenny Lind before the American public. Here he describes her first appearance in the USA under his aegis:

A thousand tickets were sold the first day, bringing in 10,141 dollars. In order to prevent confusion the doors were opened at five o'clock, although the concert did not commence until eight. The consequence was that although 5,000 persons were present at the first concert, their entrance was marked with as much order and quiet as was ever witnessed in the assembling of a congregation at church ... The reception of Jenny Lind on her first appearance, in point of enthusiasm, was probably never before equalled in the world. As Mr Benedict led her towards the footlights the entire audience rose to their feet and welcomed her with three cheers, accompanied by the waving of thousands of hats and handkerchiefs ... Towards the last portion of the cavatina (*Casta Diva*) the audience were so completely carried away by their feelings that the remainder of the air was drowned in a perfect tempest of acclamation. Enthusiasm had been wrought to its highest pitch. Her triumph was complete. At the conclusion of the concert Jenny Lind was loudly called for, and was obliged to appear three times before the audience could be satisfied.

She stayed in America for two years, travelling thousands of miles by train and paddlesteamer, singing in innumerable cities and towns. Barnum was ingenious both at crowd-pulling and at star-protection. When Jenny could not leave the ship at New Orleans because of the crowd, he disguised his own daughter

At this theatre in New York (later burned to the ground) Jenny Lind made her American debut, the first of a series of highly-popular performances under the management of the greatest showman of the day— perhaps of any day—P T Barnum. Later, his excesses shocked her, and she completed her tour of America under her own, less successful, management.

as 'the Swedish Nightingale' and used her as a decoy, while the star slipped away unnoticed. In Cincinatti, he took the deception a stage further, since the same trick would not work again. He walked down the gangway with Jenny herself while an accomplice shouted, 'You can't pass your daughter off as Jenny Lind this time!' The mob laughed and let them through, waiting patiently for the 'real' star to emerge.

But halfway through her American visit Jenny Lind ended her association with Barnum: his arrangements had always half amused, half shocked her. She became her own–and less successful–touring management. Her private life was happier. It had blossomed with the arrival of Otto Goldsmith to accompany her; they married in 1852, and returned to England where they settled. Jenny Lind inclined more and more towards sacred music and in 1883 became Professor of Singing at the Royal College of Music in London. All her life she had given away her earnings to those who needed them: she was an icon to goodness and artistry.

But if Lola Montez was the reverse, Elise Rachel was a combination of these two that thoroughly titillated her Victorian audience. She was a scarlet woman, both in the characters she played and in her life, but as an artist she was irreproachable. Rachel was the first of a very small group of international stage-actresses (Ristori, Bernhardt, Duse) who were not limited by their native tongue. Her progress round the world was abetted by the snobbishness of her audience who would always pretend to understand French, the language of culture. All her audiences pretended, save the Americans. This account of Rachel in the *New World* is written by Léon Beauvallet, a member of her touring company:

> Suddenly a strange noise, totally unexpected, almost drowns the voices of the actors. It is as if a dreadful storm has broken and the rain is pattering furiously on all the windows in the theatre. But not at all! The noise comes from the innumerable texts of the play, translated into English, which the whole audience turns over simultaneously as soon as they reach the bottom of the page. Nothing could be more comical than to hear this sudden rustling bang in the middle of a declamatory passage. Amusing, too, to notice the perfect unison in which all these pages are turned–like a regiment in evening dress executing a military command.

Rachel's début as an international actress was engineered by the ubiquitous Benjamin Lumley who invited her to London in 1841, thus precipitating her whole international career, for she took it by storm. She was a great favourite with the aristocracy and royalty who showered her with presents. There was a very venal side to Rachel. Queen Victoria presented her with a bracelet composed of two wreathed serpents with diamond heads. An anonymous and frequently catty contemporary biographer of Rachel, Mme de B–, records the actress's response:

> But it was neither the inscription nor the honor the gift brought that occupied the attention of the recipient, her mind was set on more substantial advantages. She has herself owned that her first impulse was to *feel* the *weight* of the bracelet and thence estimate its *metallic* value!

Apart from the Queen, her admirers included Benjamin Lumley, who is supposed to have proposed to her, Disraeli and the Duke of Wellington. It gave her new status at home as well as abroad: on returning to Paris she began a liaison with Count Walewski, the illegitimate son of Napoleon, whose mother was the Polish Countess Walewska. Rachel had a son by Count Walewski in 1844.

After the London début, her frequent return visits to London and tours to Belgium and Holland were equally successful, except in 1848, the year of the Revolutions. With her tunnel vision limited to her own financial prospects, Rachel summarizes the momentous period of French history in a letter from Liège–'The Republic is costing me dearly,' she wrote. In Brussels, Charlotte Brontë saw her perform and described her as 'pale like twilight, wasted like wax flame'. But she was as repelled as attracted by the experience:

> Rachel's acting thrilled me with horror. That tremendous force with which she expresses the very worst passions in their strongest essence forms an exhibition as exciting as the bullfights of Spain and the gladiatorial combats of old Rome, and (it seems to me) not one whit more moral.

Throughout her career Rachel went where she was paid the most. Mme de B– says baldly, 'Her idol was gold,' and the result was that after every absence her Parisian audience took umbrage. Whenever she returned to Paris 'it required all her talent and an extraordinary degree of exertion on her part to reconquer her place'. It must have been a salutary–and difficult–experience to come back to earth after her tour to Russia in 1854 which surpassed every triumph she had known before. Rachel wrote:

> I assure you that one needs a strong head to resist such things; all the flatteries I am told, all the incense I breathe, make complete the life of an ambitious artist. Neither Talma nor Mars, my great predecessors in public favour, ever received anything like it.

She was literally treated like a queen: 'Not like a pasteboard monarch in a tragedy with a crown of gilt cardboard, but like a real sovereign, the true minted article.'

Elise Rachel as Valeria. She was one of the greediest actresses who travelled the world in search of the highest rewards, but sometimes found travel frightening, writing in the 1850s, 'When one gets out of a train safe and sound, one can count oneself lucky, for it is inconceivable how few precautions are taken to avoid accidents.' but she died in her bed, although much too young.

In St Petersburg her performance in *Adrienne Lecouvreur* earned her a pelisse of the most costly furs in the world from the Empress, and from 'the Munificent Nicholas' a diamond and ruby corsage of great value; in addition, the box-office takings were enormous. For once, even Rachel seems to have been sated. Occasionally generosity alternated with her greed, and on this occasion she gave a large percentage of her profit to the poor and to the theatre.

In 1855 she crossed the Atlantic, but without the good offices of Barnum, her arrival was rather a low-key event. Madame de B– claims that Rachel's Jewish family 'incessantly dinned into her ears the 1,700,000 francs realised by Jenny Lind in thirty-eight nights'. She continues (in her normal lightly anti-Semitic vein), 'But these children of Israel were so completely carried away, American dollars shone so brightly before their dazzled eyes, they could not perceive how little connection existed between the easy gains made in a foreign land by a singer or a dancer and those made by a tragic actress.' Actually, with cleverer financial manipulation Rachel's visit could have rivalled Jenny Lind's, for quite spontaneously there sprung up Rachel cigars, night caps, pudding *à la Rachel*, the Rachel polka and much more. But quite apart from their disconcerting habit of following the text in translation, the reception from the American audience was disappointing, as Léon Beauvallet noted:

Rachel in America! To us that had seemed something unbelievable, splendid, marvellous! To our way of thinking it was an event that should have stirred the whole of the new continent. Rachel in America! Why, even the Indian tribes in their wild forests ought to have been discussing it! Instead of which she was received in the same fashion as a score of other artists.

Part of the magic of Rachel was the febrile quality which Charlotte Brontë noted: it was a symptom of the tuberculosis that was to kill her. She suffered from a persistent cough on the American tour, and by the time they reached Philadelphia she was in a state of collapse. The rest of the engagement was cancelled. Less than three years later she was dead. She fought desperately against the progress of her disease, which revealed to her the pathetic transience of fame. This letter to a friend, written 'by the side of the Pyramids', ought to be required reading for anyone entering the theatrical profession:

> I have lived gluttonously. I have devoured in a few years all my days and nights; well, it is done now and I do not say like your penitents: I am guilty . . . Oh my friend, here I see the empty fate of actresses. I thought I was like a pyramid and I see now that I am no more than a passing shadow–a past shadow.

There was no immediate successor to Elise Rachel: Sarah Bernhardt (1845–1923) was to inherit the crown. As unconventional, difficult and greedy as Rachel, she used the occasion of her first tour to London to get full shares in the Comédie Française company. She was a young actress but she was aware of her worth: John Murray, an eye-witness to her international début, considered she received the greatest ovation in the history of English theatre. Actually, Sarcey, a French critic familiar with Sarah's *Phèdre*, was not impressed with her performance that night. But Sarah discovered, as Rachel had before her, that a foreign audience, once it had opted to admire her, was far more easily pleased than its Parisian equivalent.

Like Rachel, Sarah was socially fêted in London and asked to all the best houses–where, incidentally, she received large fees for dining and then reciting. Even her own sculptures and works of art were exhibited: the Prince and Princess of Wales and Mr Gladstone came to the opening. She was a magnet to the press, who loved her eccentricities and extensively reported her visit to the zoo in Liverpool. There she acquired a cheetah, six chameleons and a white wolfhound to add to the bizarre menagerie already inhabiting her London lodgings. She was as hyperactive as Rachel, and as a result both her health and her work suffered. However, the undiscriminating British public never noticed–she was simply and satisfactorily a shooting star on their horizon.

The artist Sir William Nicholson chose the greatest men and women of his day for his 'portraits' and the queen of the stage was without doubt Sarah Bernhardt.

When she returned to Paris after all this adulation, the French press and public were not responsive. She did not win them back as Rachel had done, she quarrelled with the Comédie and left the company. Her success in London gave her the weapon that 'abroad' would always appreciate her, and the knowledge marked the start of a lifelong touring career. She went back to London for the second time and on this occasion critics on both sides of the Channel were unanimous in their praise. She went on to Brussels and Copenhagen where she was afraid her extreme thinness would disappoint 'those magnificent men and those splendid healthy women'. But the public was ecstatic and the Kings and Queens of Greece and Denmark threw bouquets.

At this time the impresario William Jarrett approached

Sarah about the possibility of an American tour as he had done several times before. She had always turned him down, but now she capitulated and the result was an enormous welcome for her in New York. She had to fake a fainting fit to escape the crowds. Tickets were sold by auction *à la* Jenny Lind. *La Dame aux Camélias* practically sent the press and the public into orbit: she took twenty-seven curtain calls. Her own account of her final matinée in New York, recalls Barnum's protection of Jenny Lind, and possibly marks the birth of autograph mania:

Oh, that matinee of Saturday, December 8th! I can never forget it! When I got to the theater to dress it was midday, for the matinee was to commence at half past one. My carriage stopped, not being able to get along, for the street was filled by ladies, sitting on chairs which they had borrowed from the neighboring shops, or on folding seats which they had brought themselves. The play was 'La Dame aux Camélias'. I had to get out of my carriage and walk about twenty-five yards on foot in order to get to the stage door. It took me twenty-five minutes to do it. People shook my hands and begged me to come back. One lady took off her brooch and pinned it in my mantle–a modest brooch of amethysts surrounded by fine pearls, but certainly for the giver the brooch had its value. I was stopped at every step. One lady pulled out her notebook and begged me to write my name. The idea took like lightning. Small boys under the care of their parents wanted me to write my name on their cuffs. My arms were full of small bouquets which had been pushed into my hands. I felt behind me some one tugging at the feather in my hat. I turned round sharply. A woman with a pair of scissors in her hand had tried to cut off a lock of my hair, but she had only succeeded in cutting the feather out of my hat. In vain Jarrett signalled and shouted–I could not get along. They sent for the police, who delivered me, but without any ceremony, either for my admirers or for myself. They were real brutes, those policemen, and made me very angry. I played 'La Dame aux Camélias' and I counted seventeen calls after the third act and twenty-nine after the fifth. In consequence of the cheering and calls the play had lasted an hour longer than usual and I was half dead with fatigue. I was just about to go to my carriage to get back to my hotel when Jarrett came to tell me that there were more than 50,000 people waiting outside. I fell back on a chair, tired and disheartened.

'Oh, I will wait till the crowd has dispersed! I am tired out. I can do no more.'

But Henry Abbey had an inspiration of genius.

'Stay,' said he to my sister, 'put on madame's hat and boa and take my arm. And take also these bouquets–give me what you cannot carry. And now we will go to your sister's carriage and make our bow.'

The background looks like a room but in fact it is Bernhardt's own salon in the train in which she travelled Europe.

He said all this in English and Jarrett translated it to my sister who lent herself to this little comedy very willingly. During this time Jarrett and I got into Abbey's carriage, which was stationed in front of the theater where no one was waiting. And it was fortunate we took this course, for my sister only got back to the Albemarle Hotel an hour later, very tired, but very much amused. Her resemblance to myself, my hat, my boa, and the darkness of night had been the accomplices of the little comedy which we had offered to my enthusiastic public.

She went on to Boston where she was attacked because of her repertoire and behaviour. Although this was twenty-five years after Rachel, attitudes to the 'immorality' of actresses had not loosened up: 'There were no young girls present,' said Sarah, 'as the piece was too immoral. Poor *Adrienne Lecouvreur!*' In Montreal she nearly drowned hopping on ice-floes in the St Lawrence river. Mr Jarrett feared for his investment: 'If you had lost your life, madam, you would have been dishonest for you would have broken your contract of your own free will.'

Sometimes even Sarah's ingenious manipulation of her own publicity backfired. Also in Montreal she was persuaded to inspect an iced and salted whale, and to pull a piece of shattered bone from its mouth. She was pursued thereafter by men wearing sandwich-boards with the following inscription:

Come and see the enormous cetacean which Sarah Bernhardt killed by tearing out its whalebone for her corsets.

Her attitude to Americans oscillated between keen criticism–the importunity of reporters, the dirty and over-zealous hands of customs officials–and eulogy. The women of America earned her unstinting admiration, as did Mr Edison; theatres were, after all, among the earliest users of electricity. He entertained her to supper at 3 a.m. and she thought he had much in common with Napoleon: her highest form of praise. Her tour made her the most famous actress in the New World, having considerably added to her reputation and her fortune.

Before she left Paris again she began an affair with Jacques Damala, a failed diplomat of notable indiscretion, and now a novice actor. He was dazzlingly handsome and completely without talent. She took him on in her company, and, the American foray having whetted an appetite always keen for travel, she set out for Holland, Scandinavia and Russia. She must see as well as be seen. She needed the stimulus of new places and new faces. (Not even the dangers engendered by the war, nor later the loss of her leg could arrest her desire to travel, which seemed to increase with advancing years.) From St Petersburg the company moved on to Warsaw, Austria and Italy. There, in Naples, she decided to marry Damala. They hurried together to London to marry at St Andrew's Church on 4 April 1882. He was ten years her junior and a morphine addict. The marriage was doomed and is worth noting primarily because in a life of promiscuity and illegitimate parenthood she never married anyone else.

In 1886 Sarah again crossed the Atlantic; during the next few years she was to extend her sway as far as Australia and Peru, to play in Hawaii and East Africa. But always she had to return to Paris to consolidate her hold over French audiences. She came to understand better than Rachel that to lose Paris was to lose her power abroad. By 1893 she was back in Paris to stay, richer and more famous than ever, and her audience uncharacteristically forgave her her success. Jules Lemaître wrote, 'She has been given homage in all lands of the earth, with welcome not given even to kings.'

Oswald Stoll was the owner and impresario of the Coliseum in London, and in 1910 he asked the ageing Sarah Bernhardt to play there alongside traditional music hall turns. She cabled him: 'Not after the monkeys.' In fact elephants preceded her, but Sarah was charmed by a record salary of £1,000 a week and a red carpet from her dressing-room to the stage. Aged seventy, she played a youth of nineteen in an extract from *L'Aiglon*. A war-horse of the theatre ('I will die on stage; it is my battlefield'), she returned for four more years even after her leg had been amputated. Listing her favourite things about London, Sarah included the Tower, the Crystal Palace, the Houses of Parliament and the Albert Memorial–'but you happen to have only one woman of genius on your stage, and that is Marie Lloyd'.

Marie Lloyd was much put out by being excluded from the Royal Command Performance and set out on a series of foreign tours. One of these unhappily included a stay on Ellis Island, USA.

Oswald Stoll, the owner of the Coliseum theatre in London, invited Marie Lloyd to play there but changed his mind. He was after a knighthood, too, and when he was put in charge of the Royal Command Performance, he considered her innuendos unsuitable for Queen Victoria's ears.

But Marie Lloyd never played at the Coliseum. Oswald Stoll was prey to a terrible refinement and found her music hall act, full of devastating innuendo as it was, too earthy for his premises. Born in 1870, the daughter of a waiter, Marie had triumphed in all the leading music halls in England, famed for such songs as 'My Old Man Said Follow The Van' and 'Oh, Mr Porter'. When attacked for the vulgarity of her lyrics she won her audience's hearts by amending the line 'She sits among the cabbages and peas' to 'She sits among the cabbages and leeks'. The public loved her, and when Oswald Stoll was put in charge of a Royal Command Performance there was uproar because she was not included in the programme. The fastidious Stoll did not consider her act suitable for royalty. Marie was bitterly and publicly humiliated. Playing down the road at the London Pavilion, she defiantly billed herself as *Queen of Comedy* and plastered strips across the posters proclaiming:

Every performance by Marie Lloyd is a command performance by order of the British Public

The royal rebuff was a powerful incentive for Marie to leave England. She had already made an international reputation for herself in South Africa and Australia. In 1896, aged only twenty-six, she had triumphed in South Africa, receiving among other rewards the imaginative, but somehow disappointing, present from a diamond millionaire of a box of kippers from England. In 1901 she travelled with her lover Alec Hurley (calling themselves Mr and Mrs Hurley) to play in Melbourne. They were a huge success with the Australians, who loved Marie's no-nonsense humour. Together they bought race-horses, wore fashionable clothes, gave extravagant parties and generally titillated the public. So in 1913 a tour to America seemed the ideal antidote to Oswald Stoll's neglect.

Encouraged by the success of travelling under a marital name on her previous expedition, Marie set sail as Mrs Dillon, travelling with her lover Bernard Dillon, although she was technically married to Hurley by now. She had expected to repeat the Australian experience but the reality was closer to the moral outrage which had greeted the adulterous shipboard passage of Lola Montez. On arrival they were refused entry to America by immigration and interned on Ellis Island, due to be deported back to England. She was charged with 'moral turpitude' and Dillon (under the White Slave Act of America) 'with taking to the country a woman who is not his wife'. Removed under close arrest, Marie Lloyd was reported as being (understandably) 'hysterical'. She wrote afterwards about the Statue of Liberty:

What irony! The statue ought to be pulled down. It is a standing lie. As for Ellis Island, it is horrible, horrible, horrible! Why! I wouldn't put pigs there. There is not an atom of comfort and the stench is overwhelming . . . I went raving mad and had to be attended by the doctor. I really thought I should die.

Expressions of sympathy poured in from England but the *New York Globe* remained implacable in its view of the whole business: '. . . a sense of public decency, which we trust is not lacking in England, forbids the flaunting of one's immmorality in public. That is all there is to this very disagreeable affair.'

Marie and Dillon boarded the *Olympic* to return to England and Marie issued the statement: 'I have decided never again to appear before the American public.' However, just as the ship was about to sail, they were offered bail and permission to stay, provided they lived in 'separate establishments'. Marie ate her words, presumably aided by the prospect of $1,500 a week, and when she opened in New York the stewards from the *Olympic* crowded the gallery.

It was a successful tour but not a happy one. One is irresistibly reminded of Lola Montez's propensity to attack those who dared criticize her, and there is a real sense of *déjà vu* in reading Daniel Farson's account of the tour, in his book *Marie Lloyd and Music Hall*:

> In Alberta she is supposed to have horsewhipped an editor who wrote that she talked like a scrubwoman and looked like a grandmother. She left his office with the angry promise that she would be remembered long after he was forgotten. But crowds followed her everywhere . . . They know the Queen when they see one. Queen of Variety, don't you know!

Anna Pavlova (1882–1931) was the undisputed international queen of the ballet and her motivation for her extensive travels is widely recognized as an irreproachable dedication to the dance. One of the few dissenters to this view, Dr AK Graves, contends in his autobiography of spying that she was paid 50,000 roubles a year by the Russian government. Certainly her role as ambassadress of the dance would have provided the perfect 'cover', but probably the power of the rumour relied for its potency on its incongruity. It is, after all, an amusing antidote to the perfection of the Pavlova legend to speculate that she might have been a Russian spy.

Aged ten, Pavlova joined the Imperial Ballet School in St Petersburg. By 1906 she was a fully fledged ballerina, and in 1907 Fokine created *The Dying Swan* for her: the ballet that has imprinted her on public consciousness ever since. During the following year, on her first foreign tour with the Imperial Ballet to Riga, Stockholm, Copenhagen, Helsinki, Prague and Berlin, Pavlova realized the excitement she could arouse in audiences previously ignorant of ballet. She asked her maid why the audiences were so enthusiastic, and received the reply, 'You have made them happy by letting them forget for one hour the

Images of Pavlova like this one carried her fame across the world, but in addition she herself toured to the ends of the earth for a decade, even playing to empty houses in Cuba where the potential audience was instead playing its part in revolution.

sadnesses of life'. This perception of herself as a panacea for sorrow was the fulcrum of Pavlova's ambition. She was not deterred even by the philistinism of a certain English impresario around the time of her London début soon after this. He asked her what she did, and told her to bring her tights along the next day for an audition. It did not augur well for the prospects of ballet in London!

However, by 1912, having danced regularly and successfully in London in the intervening years, she decided to settle there. She bought Ivy House in North End Road, Hampstead, sent to Russia for her possessions, and threw herself into two acres of garden and an English country-house way of life. It was not enough. In 1913 she formed her own company which was to tour to the ends of the earth for a decade. For the whole of the First World War she and her manager-husband Victor Dandré toured North and South America: once they were on that side of the Atlantic it was not easy to get back through the torpedoes, and Pavlova felt she could not risk the lives of her company. Ivy House remained the image of home: the Russian Revolution of 1917 meant the Russia she had known would never return.

The Latin America tour of 1917 started in Cuba, where they played to empty houses for three weeks during the Revolution. The members of the company were paid only $3 a day, to include hotels and food. The only way to beat a retreat was by cattle-boat to Ecuador, sleeping on deck because of the heat.

When they arrived in Guayaquil they danced to a ragged peasant audience, with the exception of a few opulent English cocoa-merchants in the boxes. They were enthusiastically received, save for reservations about the indecency of the costumes. The locals disapproved of the ballerinas' bare arms and necks, and the exposure of so much leg. Worst of all, the men wore no hats. The company must have given off some aura of respectability, however, for when they sailed away from South America a bishop wrote to the ship's captain asking for special protection for Pavlova and her group. She might have been glad of it in Mexico City, where she was so popular that she had to give extra performances in a bull-ring. It rained, Pavlova was forced to stop dancing, and a major riot ensued. A compensation in the same city was when Pablo Casals unexpectedly accompanied her in her *Swan Solo*. Recognizing him, she danced towards him with her eyes so wide with surprise that he was forced to shut his in order to continue playing.

Theodore Stier, Pavlova's Austrian musical director for sixteen years, reckoned that from 1913 to 1923 they travelled 300,000 miles, he conducted 3,650 performances and 2,000 rehearsals. The facilities were often rudimentary, but Pavlova liked dancing in improbably far-off places where ballet had never been seen before. In Rangoon she was billed as 'The Sensation of All The Civilized World', and it did not seem to matter that the musicians were not trained to play Western music. In Montgomery, Alabama, the roof leaked and there were puddles on the stage but Pavlova's comment was: 'Never mind—these are the people who need me and it gives me more joy to dance for them than at the Metropolitan Opera House.'

Unlike most of her predecessors in this chapter, even Jenny Lind, Pavlova was very dignified in her attitude to publicity. She gave restrained interviews to the press, but she definitely shied from contact with her adoring public. In contrast to Sarah Bernhardt's dining and reciting, Pavlova once offered to reduce her fee from £500 to £300 if she were not obliged to take dinner with the guests at a social function where she was to dance. She did, however, take her obligation to a new generation of dancers very seriously and never shirked seeing girls who wanted advice. Apart from the odd startling dividend, like Tamara Toumanova who was inspired to become a dancer after seeing Pavlova in Shanghai, it must have been generally a dispiriting business. It led Pavlova to occasional outbursts, such as this one to a teacher of dance in Denver, Colorado: 'Here is no talent and a method which is totally wrong ... Not only are you incompetence personified but you are spoiling years of these children's lives.'

If she was tireless for her art, she was also a tireless sightseer. In the mass of testimony to her dedication to the dance, it is refreshing to read that she frequently skipped the daily company class to go to the art galleries of Florence, take a boat to Benares, climb the Sphinx, ride a camel to the Pyramids. But ballet permeated everything she did: after nearly being snowed up in a mountain pass, a high sunny valley in California filled with yellow poppies gave her the inspiration for her dance *The Californian Poppy*. When she died in 1931 she was mourned in every country where she had ever danced.

Isadora Duncan (1878–1927) possessed the same sort of driving artistic ambition as Pavlova, wishing to spread the gospel of her own kind of dance to new lands and new generations, but her single-mindedness was hampered by a marked capacity for erotic adventure. 'My life has known but two motives,' she wrote, 'Love and Art–and often Love destroyed Art and often the imperious call of Art put a tragic end to Love.' She recognized the gulf between her attitude to dance and Pavlova's, and records their meeting in St Petersburg in 1905 in this extract from her autobiography *My Life*:

> After supper the indefatigable Pavlowa [sic] danced again, to the delight of her friends. Although it was five o'clock in the morning before we left, she invited me to come at half-past eight the same morning, if I would like to see her work. I arrived three hours later (I confess I was considerably fatigued) to find her standing in her tulle dress practising at the bar, going through the most rigorous gymnastics, while an old gentleman with a violin marked the time, and admonished her to greater efforts. This was the famous master Petitpas [sic].
>
> For three hours I sat tense with bewilderment, watching the amazing feats of Pavlowa. She seemed to be made of steel and elastic. Her beautiful face took on the stern lines of a martyr. She never stopped for one moment. The whole tendency of this training seems to be to separate the gymnastic movements of the body completely from the mind. The mind, on the contrary, can only suffer aloofness from this rigorous muscular discipline. This is just the opposite from all the theories on which I founded my school, by which the body becomes transparent and is a medium for the mind and spirit.

Isadora was extremely serious about her own form of dance. San Francisco-born, she made her first foray abroad to London in 1899, where she earned a precarious living by giving private recitals: 'One day I would find myself dancing before Royalty, or in the garden at Lady Lowther's, and the next with nothing to eat. For sometimes I was paid, more often I was not.' Despite her financial situation she could not be seduced like Bernhardt had been into appearing at a music hall. Her lofty ideals led her to rebuff the offer of a German impresario in no uncertain terms:

> 'No,' I said, 'my Art is not for a music-hall. I will come to Berlin some day, and I hope to dance to your Philharmonic Orchestra, but in a Temple of Music, not in a music-hall with

A photograph of Isadora Duncan, taken by her lover Edward Gordon Craig. He was a highly talented stage designer. For him, Isadora missed performances and abandoned her friends. But in the end, although she was the mother of his child, her career triumphed and they parted.

acrobats and trained animals. Quelle horreur! Mon Dieu! No, not on any terms. I bid you good day and adieu.'

Looking at our surroundings and shabby clothes, this German impresario could hardly believe his ears. When he returned the next day, and the next, and finally offered me a thousand marks an evening for one month, he grew very angry, and characterised me as a 'Dummes Mädel', until finally I shouted at him that I had come to Europe to bring about a great renaissance of religion through the Dance, to bring the knowledge of the Beauty and Holiness of the human body through its expression of movements, and not to dance for the amusement of overfed bourgeoisie after dinner.

It was the Russian visit of 1905 where not only Pavlova but Stanislavsky and Bakst provided her with the heady appreciation that gave Isadora the impetus to establish a school intended to perpetuate her ideal of the dance. At Grünewald, Berlin, she and her sister Elizabeth corralled a random selection of children, surrounded them with artistic references to dance and movement, set them on a rigid programme of gymnastics and fed them a vegetarian diet. Given this stoic regime, it is not surprising that Isadora soon succumbed to one of her regular sins of the flesh. She met the volatile young theatre designer Edward Gordon Craig, son of Ellen Terry, who displayed a definite sense of décor even in the consummation of their relationship:

Craig then took me up to his studio at the top of a high building in Berlin. There was a black, waxed floor with rose-leaves strewn all over it.

Here stood before me brilliant youth, beauty, genius; and, all inflamed with sudden love, I flew into his arms with all the magnetic willingness of a temperament which had for two years lain dormant, but waiting to spring forth. Here I found an answering temperament, worthy of my metal. In him I had met the flesh of my flesh, the blood of my blood. Often he cried to me, 'Ah, you are my sister.'

I do not know how other women remember their lovers. I suppose it is the correct thing to stop always at a man's head, shoulders, hands, etc., and then describe his clothes, but I always see him, as that first night in the studio, when his white, lithe, gleaming body emerged from the chrysalis of clothes and shone upon my dazzled eyes in all his splendour.

She was so overwhelmed that she stayed with him for two weeks. It was definitely a case of Love triumphing over Art; her impresario was wild with worry, as she missed performances; her mother was frantic and visited every embassy and police station. She bore Craig's child in 1906, but by 1907 she was back on tour in Russia, London and New York, revelling in popular and critical acclaim. Art was back on the agenda, and she became obsessed with the idea of taking her school to different countries in order to tempt each government to recognize the beauty of her project and to inject some much needed capital: '. . . audiences looked upon me and my school as a charming amusement, but I could find no real aid for the foundation of a future school.'

Soon Isadora's own resources ran out: 'As always the expenses of my little flock were enormous . . . Once more my bank account was nil.'

The problem was solved in typical Isadora style. She voiced the opinion that a millionaire was what she needed, and on her return to Paris in 1909 she met and captivated one, Paris Singer, whom she dubbed 'Lohengrin'. He bore the expenses of installing her 'little flock' in a villa on the Riviera, dismissed the diamond-clad woman in his life and won the love of Isadora. To be sure, both Art and her devotion to Singer faltered when Craig appeared to see her after a performance:

> . . . for a short moment I was on the verge of believing that nothing mattered, neither the school nor Lohengrin nor anything–but just the joy of seeing him again. However, a dominant trait in my character is fidelity.

Only four pages on in her autobiography she is making passionate love to her accompanist. Singer never knew of it, but despite the birth of a son, their relationship soon broke up because of his jealousy over what was, according to Isadora, an innocent friendship: 'In spite of our innocence Lohengrin was never convinced of it and swore he would never see me again.' When he relented sufficiently to ask to see his son and Craig's daughter, of whom he was very fond, a terrible tragedy temporarily united the couple. On their return from seeing Singer, the children and their nurse were involved in a car accident and all three were drowned in the Seine. Isadora could find no consolation:

> If this sorrow had come to me much earlier in life I might have overcome it; if much later it would not have been so terrible; but at that moment in the full power and energy of life it completely shattered my force and power.

Singer proved inadequate–'If a great love had then enveloped me and carried me away . . . but Lohengrin did not respond to my call'–but Art helped to heal the wounds. The tragedy made her redouble her efforts to set up her schools, and she continued to lay siege for funds. In 1916 she made a remarkable tour of South America. Her accompanist, Maurice Dumesnil, recorded their picaresque travels in his book *An Amazing Journey* and by the time they reached Buenos Aires he was feeling critical:

I will admit frankly that Isadora was spoiled . . . She was used to having everybody worship at her shrine and took it as an insult if anyone ever attempted to act differently.

Buenos Aires did not react well to Isadora, nor she to it:

It was like casting pearls before swine . . . They don't know anything. They're nothing but a bunch of niggers.

But she was a triumph in Montevideo, and squired by so many attractive young men that Dumesnil lost track of her activities. Rio, after a slow start, proved a sensation–the morning daily *O Paiz* pushed the war off the front page and devoted three columns to 'Isadora, the divine'.

Plainly Isadora was regaining her lust for life; in his pained way Dumesnil records the conquests in every town. She even made them on the train. 'You know,' said Isadora, 'in Brazil they are ahead of the whole world when it comes to sleeping car accommodations. Their lay-out system is ideal. The idea of that washroom when there is pleasant company the other side–why it's simply genial.'

In 1921 she was at last invited by the Soviet government to found a school in Moscow. It was a disappointing period. It proved a desperate struggle to maintain the school at a time of privation in Russia. She became a somewhat hysterical Leninist in her determination for the cause, but was mocked by the Russians themselves. Most disappointing was her marriage to the young poet, Sergei Alexandrevitch Essenine. He was no appreciator of her art: when he first saw her dance he was coarsely offensive.

Isadora Duncan had a profound effect on the history of dancing because she was not only a great innovator but determined to teach the world, particularly the young of the world, her art. Within five years of the Russian Revolution she was invited by Lenin to open the Moscow School of Dancing, the world centre of dance. Unfortunately it failed, but she continued to proselytize until her death in 1927.

The friend who was acting as interpreter said with evident hesitation to Isadora: 'He says it was–awful . . . and that he can do better than that himself.' And even before the whole speech was translated to the crestfallen and humiliated Isadora, the poet was on his feet dancing about the studio like a crazy man.

It was a masochistic relationship for Isadora: she gave, and he took and destroyed. In her final touring days he made her life hell, bullying, drinking, wrecking hotels, spoiling her galas, stealing her possessions. She still drew audiences all over Europe even as she became fat, depressed and alcoholic. The suddenness of her death was of a piece with her life: a trailing scarf (which was part of the loose, flowing dress she always affected) caught in the wheel of a car and she was strangled on the Promenade des Anglais in Nice, while still planning for the future of her dance.

CHAPTER 3

MISSIONARIES

Kate Marsden wrapped herself up well for the fearful journey ahead. She says that when a girl held up a mirror, laughing at her, she failed to recognise herself. Behind her in this studio portrait, is a map of Russia showing her route across Siberia where it was rumoured that in Yatusk, she would find a herb which alleviated the fearful suffering of the lepers. Her journey– 2000 miles on horseback–took eleven months.

The conventional image of a nineteenth-century woman missionary is of a battle-axe full of moral and physical courage but lacking in imagination. The virtue of heroism is somehow cancelled by narrow-mindedness. But the pioneers of foreign missions totally contradict this impression, for bigotry and travel can rarely survive side by side for long. Women working abroad soon mitigated their religious zeal into a practical humanitarianism: bodies were tackled before souls. Kate Marsden handed out packets of tea and sugar to Siberian prisoners before producing her copies of the New Testament, and because their clothing was inadequate for sub-zero temperatures she took off her own warm sheepskins–'My furs would almost have burnt me had I gone to the poor creatures thus clad.' Mary Slessor, the 'White Ma' of Calabar, opened up the trading and brought prosperity to the people of Okoyong before she tackled the superstition and barbarism which horrified her. The missionaries were capable, too, of modifying their initial view of heathenism. Henrietta Streatfield, working with the Zenana Missionaries in South India, was initially shocked and repelled by spirit-worship, 'which makes one thankful to be born in a Christian country'. The habits of the hill tribe of Todas horrified her:

> One young Toda woman whom I saw had already changed her husband four times; and she was only twenty! There is no morality whatever among them, and they seem almost savage in their way of living.

But in the relatively brief span of her work in India she came to realize that she must try to understand the existing culture of her converts and try to build on that rather than destroy it. She recognized 'an innate devoutness in the Hindoo mind' and, abandoning the hidebound certainty with which she had left home, she acknowledged that the religious instinct was much more developed in the East than in the West.

The energies of the missionaries were harnessed to a cause which enabled them to rise above physical hardship and disability. Like Kate Marsden, Annie Taylor had suffered from consumption, but she crossed the high passes of Tibet in an epic journey of endurance involving wolves, brigands and betrayal, fortified by her determination to open up Tibet to Christianity. Mary Moffat and Mary Livingstone put up with unremitting pregnancies and somehow reared families in the African bush while carrying out risky pioneer missionary duties.

Many of these women were unique and inspiring personalities who would have been misfits in their own society, which demanded subordination and convention of their sex. Mildred Cable and Evangeline and Francesca French, the three-in-one (appropriately enough in view of their calling), spent fifteen years crossing and re-crossing the Gobi desert five times. In England they would have mouldered as a trio of eccentric old maids–for them missionary work was an acceptable path to independence. Mary Slessor 'went native', protected by the respectability of her calling, and departed from all established orders of procedure following ideals, not rules. In time, their individualism even earned them respect. The privately printed biographical memoir of the beautiful militant suffragist Dr Helen Hanson is defensive but admiring of her eccentricities. She emerged as a quirky and fascinating woman, strongly religious but capable of dashing off *A Critical Dissertation on Urdu by OWDK (One Who Doesn't Know) (with apologies to those who do)*, which reveals her tolerant understanding of her Indian converts:

> '. . . the common people have no word for 'wait'. *Rah dekhne*, 'to look along the road', is the expression they use. They squat on their haunches and chat, or bargain, or sleep, or smoke the hookah, and why should any of these pleasant occupations be tainted by the breath of the suspicion of annoyance and irritation–to the English mind–in the word 'wait'?

Helen Hanson, a missionary with a strong sense of humour.

Her serious medical work was punctuated by jokes:

> Full many a mortal young and old
> Has gone to his sarcophagus
> By pouring water icy cold
> Adown his hot oesophagus.

Her biographer describes Helen Hanson's disregard for appearances: mismatching shoes; layers of clothes (about which she remarked it was quite distinguished to look like a balloon); eating sandwiches late at night on top of a bus; and capering round with child-like abandon at a sober Church Congress. It is a beguiling portrait that confirms the suspicion that the repressed, hidebound missionary is something of a myth.

Each of these women had a particular worth and faced a specific challenge. Mary Moffat and Mary Livingstone, the South African missionaries, were a thorn in the side of the Boers who resented their defence of tribal rights. The China Inland Mission, which included Annie Taylor early in her career and the Mildred Cable 'trio', had to battle against the intricate forces of Chinese politics and contend with the deeply ingrained demands of Confucianism, such as foot-binding and the subordination of women. Annie Taylor then faced the unique challenge of penetrating Tibet, where foreign women were not allowed, facing the likelihood of imprisonment or worse. Kate Marsden and Helen Hanson carried on a crusade against indigenous disease and the ignorance which perpetuated it. They all possessed and needed a political awareness to gain their ends. It was fortunate that they had an unworldly vision to carry them through.

Missions were often a dynastic business. The most famous mother-and-daughter pair in missionary history were Mary Smith Moffat (1795–1870), and her daughter Mary Livingstone (1820–1862), who were a powerful force in the spread of Christianity in Africa. Both worked in a marital partnership: Mary Moffat spent forty years with her husband Robert Moffat at the missionary station they built up together at Kuruman; Mary Livingstone supported her demanding and dedicated explorer husband David Livingstone in all his endeavours. The dedicated missionary wives in some ways had an even harder life than the independent spinster missionaries, for they had constantly to balance love for the family against duty to God–and the family was often sacrificed. Physically, too, they had the extra ordeal of child-birth in appalling conditions, and all too frequent infant mortality. They not only wrestled with their own health problems, but they had to create domestic self-sufficiency in the bush while carrying out their religious duties. When Mary Moffat married Robert in Cape Town in 1819, she displayed her understanding of the rules from the outset: 'Surely it ought to afford consolation that I am now united to one who counts not his life dear to himself.'

The bride's first missionary journey was by ox-drawn cart 600 miles from Cape Town to Kuruman in the interior of Cape Province. There she learned to make her home in a mud hut, and to wash her clothes in the river with the natives:

> . . . instead of rubbing they beat things upon the stones, which wears them fast. When we get settled I wish very much to wash in the English way. We cannot at present for want of tubs, but Moffat has promised to make me some, as I know he will.

She had to subscribe, however, to the African way of making soap and candles from the fat of sheep's tails, '. . . an immense and troublesome business being three weeks every day on the fire and requiring the most constant attention.' Some domestic

The most famous missionary mother is Mary Smith Moffat whose daughter was Mary Livingstone. She spent 40 years with her husband at the missionary station they built together in Africa.

tips were relayed most enthusiastically to England, however:

> I have yet another of our customs to relate. You will perhaps think it curious when I tell you that we smear all our room floors with cow dung once a week at least. At first when I saw Sister Helm do it, I thought to myself, 'But I'll do without that dirty trick, or I will try hard.' However, I had not been here long but was glad to have it done, and I have hardly patience to wait till Saturday. It lays the dust better than anything, kills the fleas which would otherwise breed abundantly, and is a fine clear green. You observe it is mixed with water, and laid on as thinly as possible. I now look upon my floor smeared with cow dung as with as much complacency as I used to do upon our best rooms when well scoured.

Spiritual progress with the natives was very slow: 'I find missionaries are greatly despised here and indeed it is not to be wondered at after the conduct of some.' The people's concept of God was as the author of everything unfortunate: 'If it rains when they don't wish it, they ask why God does so; if the ground is parched, the same.' The newly built church was empty of a congregation, children were removed from Mary's infant classes, and Mary wrote home sadly, 'Could we but see the smallest fruit, we could rejoice midst the privations and toils which we bear.' This bleak period of non-achievement was very discouraging to Robert, but Mary kept up her optimism sufficiently to send for communion plate from England–which arrived when the natives were fighting each other in a depressingly unChristian fashion. They considered themselves blessed when their first child Mary was born in 1820. 'Surely this is the Lord's doing and is wonderful in our eyes,' wrote Robert. There were to be nine more blessings, some of whom did not survive, and in addition they adopted three native children. Tribal custom demanded that children be sacrificed with a mother who died; the Moffats saved their three from burial alive. Mary's domestic burden must have been enormous, but she managed to combine it with nursing and teaching, convinced that their patient labours would eventually be rewarded.

In 1829 there came a turning-point, and in a few months the station was transformed by a wave of simultaneous enthusiasm. The church was full and the natives constantly sought instruction. Superstition receded, Christian morality took unexpected hold, cleanliness proved to be next to godliness, and to Mary's relief, 'heathen costume' was abandoned in favour of European costume. She was at last able to write to England, 'Our gracious God has been very condescending to spare the lives of his unworthy servants to witness some fruits of missionary labour,' and to feel that the condition of the mission was sufficiently hopeful for the Moffats to leave it briefly. In 1830 they travelled by ox-cart to Grahamstown, to place their two eldest children, Mary and Agnes, in the Wesleyan school there. Keeping them any longer at home would have been 'highly improper', the school was cheap and comparatively near the mission, and famous for the strict attention paid to religious instruction. Their mother saw it as her duty to part with them, but one can feel again the conflict between vocation and family in this letter to her father:

> Hence you will perceive that we are entering on a new sort of trials. We purpose calling to see them as we return, after which it is probable Moffat will be many years before he sees them again. It is likely, however, that I may come in the course of two or three years, as we have not friends to fulfil the duties of a mother to them. How happy are we, my dear friend, to have a covenant God to go to in all these straits and difficulties. Nature has its struggle, but we are not to confer with flesh and blood.

Their absence from Kuruman had a two-fold purpose: Robert continued on from Grahamstown 400 miles to Cape Town on horseback, carrying in his pocket the manuscript of parts of the New Testament that he had translated. His intention was to get it printed, but type and compositors were scarce, so Robert and a missionary colleague set to work themselves, and 'they were soon able to turn out the books in fair style [and] to regard themselves as finished apprentices'. Mary had meanwhile joined him by sea, and they returned together to their mission station to continue work tranquilly and prosperously until 1839. By this time Kuruman was a model of its kind, and the Moffats felt able to make their first trip to England since their marriage twenty years earlier. It was no longer any kind of home for them, and while Robert lectured and reported on their work, Mary yearned for Kuruman 'where we so long toiled and suffered, to see our beloved companions in the toils and sufferings and to behold our swarthy brethren and sisters again'.

When they returned to Africa they stopped at a post 150 miles from their mission, and there met the young David Livingstone, who had been inspired to become a missionary after hearing Robert Moffat speak in London. He had been mauled by a marauding lion, so the Moffats took him on with them to Kuruman to receive proper medical attention. There he was nursed by the twenty-three-year-old Mary, a situation which resulted in their engagement. The demands he would make with his prolonged absences throughout their marriage were apparent in his first letter to her: 'And now my dearest, farewell. Let your affection be towards Him much more than towards me.'

Fortunately Mary Livingstone's character had been forged by her observation of her mother's determination and by long separations from her parents. They began their life together in 1845 in a mud-hut in Mabotsa, a snake-infested area. She taught at an infants' school, as her mother had done before her, and like her mother she had to learn to manage on a missionary's

small salary–except that in the first year most of David's £100 annual wage was already spent on maintaining native teachers and buying medicines. After two years of disappointing results in Mabotsa, David decided to move on forty miles to Chonuane. Forty miles sounds deceptively little: but it was through rough, sometimes almost impenetrable, country, through unfamiliar and unfriendly villages. Mary was pregnant with her second child and nursing her sick first-born. She travelled in an ox-cart and her destination with her babies was an area of warring tribes. This, if she had but known it, was to be a foretaste of many more terrible journeys, but she was not yet hardened to the Livingstone trail, and at the prospect of crossing an apparently impassable flooded river, she burst into tears. In later years only prolonged separation from her husband could have such an effect on her. Having eventually reached Chonuane, it was to find that the corn supplies had run out, and the whole family was forced to journey on 300 miles to her parents' prudently stocked mission. Those who had known Mary were shocked by her emaciated appearance. When they returned to Chonuane, the first difficult steps in planting Christianity took a further toll on their health and spirits. A visit from Mrs Moffat in 1846 improved matters: her cheerful presence, as much as the supplies she brought, lifted the Livingstone morale–it was a source of delight to her to be reminded of her own early days at Kuruman when her positivity never failed her.

Livingstone did not often appear to show great tenderness towards his wife and children as he believed he owed his duty to a higher being, but he did ask, 'Shall I return with this or that one alive?'

But Mary Livingstone was soon alone again with her two children, while David established another home at Kolobeng. There was no more bursting into tears; David's letters indicate that she became the mistress of underrating her predicament: 'Mary feels her situation among the ruins is a little dreary and no wonder, for she writes me that the lions are resuming possession and walk around our house at night.' More wild animals abounded in the new mission at Kolobeng, and they lived in an insect-infested hut until David built another house, suffering in the process all the accidents to which the amateur builder is prone. But for the first time their missionary work prospered:

> The daily routine–up with the sun, family worship, breakfast, school, then manual work as required–ploughing, sowing, smithing and every other sort. Mary busy all the morning with culinary and other work; a rest of two hours after dinner; then she goes to the infant school with an attendance of from 60 to 80.

The tide of Boer immigration posed an impossible situation to missionaries in the area of the Orange Free State, Natal and the Transvaal, for the Boers encroached ruthlessly upon the lands and rights of many tribes, forcing them to choose between exile or slavery. It was an annoyance to the Boers that missionaries gave testimony to the outside world of what was going on, and therefore encouraged the natives to believe they had human and civil rights; they discouraged any religious presence in what they had come to regard as Boer territory. Under these circumstances Livingstone turned his attention northwards, using Kolobeng simply as a basis for operations, and began that series of explorations that absorbed the rest of his life, opening up Africa to Christianity but separating him from his wife and children. After their third child was born in 1849, Livingstone set off to unknown country and discovered Lake Ngami. Mary, pregnant again, travelled to see it, but the journey weakened her and she contracted an infection that killed her new-born baby and semi-paralysed her. She had not the physical strength to travel to the Cape for treatment but she had the inner strength to allow Livingstone to abandon her again to pursue his explorations: 'My wife, poor soul I pity her, proposed to let me go for a year while she remains at Kolobeng.'

In fact she went to her mother at Kuruman, where she made a temporary recovery which Livingstone interpreted as the capacity to accompany him to the Zambezi. His goal now was to open a passage to the sea on either the eastern or western coast of Africa. Mrs Moffat, enfeebled by illnesses of her own, could no longer summon up her old optimism:

> I cannot help contemplating what is before the Livingstones ... Thus my sympathy is excessively excited–I say excessively, but this I ascribe to my physical debility, for what I would have faced courageously (when once convinced of my duty) seems now very formidable to me.

Even Livingstone was not without fears for his children and his wife, who was pregnant again: 'A parent's heart alone can feel as I do when I look at my little ones and ask shall I return with this or that one alive?' But Mary's understanding of her duty had never been clearer, or possibly more difficult. Livingstone later wrote of her phenomenal self-discipline when the lives of their children were indeed at stake:

> The supply of water in the wagons had been wasted by one of our servants and by the afternoon only a small portion remained for the children. The idea of their perishing before our eyes was terrible. It would almost have been a relief to me to have been reproached with being the entire cause of the catastrophe, but not one syllable of upbraiding was uttered by their mother, though the tearful eye told of the agony within. In the afternoon, to our inexpressible relief, some of our men returned with a supply of that fluid of which we had never before felt the true value.

Having been left at the Chobe camp while Livingstone continued northwards, Mary gave birth to a son and was again afflicted with partial paralysis. Livingstone finally allowed his family to take precedence over his exploration, but there is something unfortunate in his expression of his dilemma to the directors of the London Missionary Society: 'Nothing but the strong conviction that the step will tend to the Glory of Christ would make me orphanise my children.' It took six months for the party to reach Cape Town, where in April 1852 Mary and the children sailed for England, leaving Livingstone to pursue his vocation. It took their separation from him to elicit an uncharacteristic note of tenderness towards his wife: 'I never show my feelings; but I can say truly, my dearest, that I loved you when I married you, and the longer I lived with you, I loved you the better.' Mary suffered very greatly during their lengthy absence from each other. She and her children lived in genteel poverty in cheap lodgings, moving from place to place. At one point she begged to be allowed to return to Africa, but either she was dissuaded by the Missionary Society on grounds of health, or she changed her mind. Livingstone endured hardships of a different kind, and in the process made

In old age, Mary Smith Moffat had the distressing experience of outliving her daughter, both of them stalwart self-sacrificing women.

such important discoveries that the map of Central Africa had to be redrawn. When he returned to England and Mary, he was lionized: he visited the Queen, the Royal Society elected him a Fellow, and he was eulogized by luminaries ranging from the Bishop of Cape Town to Charles Dickens. Paying tribute to Mary at a dinner in his honour, Livingstone said, with truth, that she had always been 'the main spoke in my wheel'.

The Livingstones set off to Africa again together, but Mary was pregnant once more and became ill at sea. Livingstone was obliged to land her at the Cape and leave her to recuperate with her parents. 'It was bitter parting with my wife,' he wrote, 'like tearing the heart out of one.' Not at any time does he seem to have acknowledged that the repeated pregnancies were gradually tearing the life out of her. Mary returned to her children with her new baby, but it was a period of intense depression and wavering of faith. In the twenty years of her marriage she had lived with her husband for only four. Finally she set off again to meet him on the Zambezi delta, where they spent six months dealing with cargo in a fever-ridden area. He was anxious to get her away from this dangerous place, but she was suddenly taken ill and after six days lapsed into a coma and died. Livingstone buried her beneath a baobab tree, in the gardens where they had walked together: 'Oh my Mary, my Mary! how often we have longed for a quiet home.'

Mrs Moffat outlived her daughter by eight years, during which time she continued to work with Robert Moffat at Kuruman. On her return to England in 1870 she died; another stalwart self-sacrificial wife, for whom her husband mourned, 'For fifty-three years I have had her to pray for me.'

In 1872 the death of David Livingstone released a flood of missionary enthusiasm, for he was by then an almost legendary figure. One of those inspired by his example was Mary Slessor, a former Scottish factory girl who in 1875 offered her services to the Foreign Mission Board, and was accepted at an annual salary of £60. For thirty-eight years she was to serve the Calabar Mission, working over a 2,000-mile area of West Africa and employing imaginative and original methods. Her biographer WP Livingstone has a whole chapter on what he calls her 'eccentricities'. The one thing essential to her was her work and anything that hampered her freedom of action was jettisoned. 'She knew that there were some people like the official who saw her pushing her canoe down to the river and preferred not to know her; but she was always sustained by the knowledge she was acting in her Master's spirit.' She sometimes mislaid Sundays. 'I lost it a fortnight ago,' she wrote, 'and kept it on a Saturday. Never mind. God will hear all the prayers and answer them all the same.' Her oddities made her a unique inspiration to others: she had all the charisma of Livingstone— but without a wife to back her up.

While not part of a missionary dynasty like the Moffats, Mary Slessor nevertheless inherited her religious enthusiasm from her mother, who had always been interested in foreign mission work. Indeed, once Mary had arrived in Calabar she told King Eyo Honesty IV of her mother's involvement, and he was so pleased that he struck up a correspondence with her. It is pleasant to contemplate the relationship across 4,000 miles of sea between an African king and an obscure Scottish woman, drawn together by the catalyst of Mary. However, it was to be away from the main mission that Mary's real work was done. As soon as she toured the outposts, she recognized that she was in touch with the foundations of any true progress. At first a 'white Ma' was so curious a sight that chieftains had to drive the crowds away from her, but gradually she became assimilated and learnt to speak the Calabar dialect of Efik. Like the most perceptive and effective of her colleagues, Mary saw that although witchcraft was practised and secret societies abounded this was not so much evidence of 'heathenism' but 'theology' of a kind on which Christian beliefs could be grafted.

Mary Slessor, one of seven children of a Scottish family, worked in a weaving shed for twelve hours a day, where her one outside interest was the Bible. Despite a chronic malarial condition, she went to Calabar where she worked just as hard to carry religion to those in 'spiritual darkness'.

If people were accustomed to canons and conventions of one kind they could be led to accept the principles of another. There were, of course, tribal customs of which she could not approve, and she is most famous for tackling head-on the superstitious practice of crushing newborn twins into jars. The naturalist Mary Kingsley, not noted for her approval of Europeans trespassing on her own patch of Africa, admired Mary Slessor from their first meeting, which happened to be the day when the first twin Susie was taken into her home:

> Miss Slessor had heard of the twins' arrival and had started off, barefooted and bareheaded, at that pace she can go down a bush path . . . All the attention one of the children wanted– the boy, for there were a boy and a girl–was burying, for the people who had crammed them into the box had utterly smashed the child's head. The other child was alive, and is

still a member of that household of rescued children, all of whom owe their lives to Miss Slessor.

The other issue which preoccupied her was that of drink–introduced by the white man–which left a trail of demoralization and ruin, just as it had in Mary's own home–her childhood experience of an alcoholic father was an excellent preparation for dealing with tribal drunkenness. WP Livingstone describes what she had to contend with:

> It was significant of the state of the district that gin, guns, and chains were practically the only articles of commerce that entered it. Gin or rum was in every home. It was given to every babe: all work was paid for with it: every fine and debt could be redeemed with it: every visitor had to be treated to it: every one drank it, and many drank it all the time. Quarrels were the outcome of it. Then the guns came into play. After that the chains and padlocks.

Mary was understandably bitter about profits made by 'civilized' countries from the sale of alcohol.

While she did not have to face the painful dilemma of family duty versus missionary duty like Mrs Moffat and Mrs Livingstone, without a family in Africa Mary suffered greatly from homesickness. 'Calabar needs a brave heart and a stout body,' she wrote; 'not that I have very much of the former, but I have felt the need for it often when sick and lonely.' Transplanted from grey Scottish skies and cool weather, she displayed tireless energy in a tropical climate where everyone tends to languor, but 'I want my home and I want my mother,' she confessed. As time went on, Calabar became the only home she knew and self-doubt was banished by her complete faith in divine providence as she explained later in *Our Faithful God: Answers to Prayer*.

> My life is one long daily, hourly, record of answered prayer. For physical health, for mental overstrain, for guidance given marvellously, for errors and dangers averted, for enmity to the Gospel subdued, for food provided at the exact hour needed, for everything that goes to make up life and my poor service, I can testify with a full and often wonder-stricken awe that I believe God answers prayer.
>
> I can give no other testimony. I am sitting alone here on a log among a company of natives. My children, whose very lives are a testimony that God answers prayer, are working round me. Natives are crowding past on the bush road to attend palavers, and I am at perfect peace, far from my own countrymen and conditions, because I know God answers prayer. Food is scarce just now. We live from hand to mouth. We have not more than will be our breakfast today, but I know we shall be fed, for God answers prayer.

After twelve years at Duke Town, Old Town and Creek Town, in 1886 Mary moved on to the district of Okoyong. As she paddled down Old Calabar River she wondered, 'Who am I, a weak woman, to face wild savages alone?' But she was as much of a pioneer as Livingstone, always wanting to go forward to reach untouched minds. Like him, she said, 'I am ready to go anywhere provided it be forward.' All the problems she had already encountered–infanticide, witchcraft, alcoholism–were rampant in this new area, but a new (and to Mary most humiliating) experience was as an inmate of the harem. Her biographer refers reticently to the 'degraded intimacies' she saw, but concludes tactfully, 'Some of the scenes she witnessed in the harem cannot be described. "Had I not felt my Saviour close beside me," she said, "I would have lost my reason." When at home the memory of these would make her wince and flush with indignation and shame. She had no patience with people who expounded the theory of the innocence of man outside the pale of civilization– she would tell them to go and live for a month in a West African harem.'

Gradually she won over the people of Okoyong–with love and wisdom and prayers to be sure, but also by practical measures. She opened up trade for them, bringing prosperity; she built schools and taught in them; she opened 'kirks' and preached in them, and, chronically ill as she was herself with recurrent malaria, she doctored them. She was an unconventional, though obviously very effective, magistrate. A government official of the time recalled that she boxed a chief's ears after he continued to interrupt after warnings–an act which caused the greatest amusement to other chiefs. When fines were imposed and the offenders had no money, she would make them work for the mission to earn the amount, and feed them well. Needless to say they became her devoted admirers. Her excuse for such irregular judicial procedures was that she might influence their lives while they were working.

She was hardly ever free from illness and pain, and yet she seemed able to do things which would have been fatal to most Europeans. She never used mosquito-netting, she never wore a hat, she went barefoot despite the prevalence of jiggers and snakes. She never boiled the water, she ate native food, and she kept most irregular hours, for she was often ministering at night and her days were taken up with long 'palavers'. When she died in 1915, in her rough-built hut in Calabar with her native family–Janie, Annie, Maggie, Alice and Whitie–about her, she left the spell of her unconventionality behind her, and the romance of her name drew many others into foreign missions.

Kate Marsden (1859–1931), the author of the arrestingly titled *On Sledge and Horseback to Outcast Siberian Lepers*, became famous as the result of the publication of her book, but more important to her, the crusade for lepers caught the public's imagination. Physically she was the most unlikely candidate for one of the most testing missionary journeys ever made. Many

women missionaries struggled with locally acquired disease, but Kate had a lifelong invalidism. She was born into a comfortably off Victorian family that was riddled with tuberculosis–only two out of the eight Marsden children survived into middle age. Only the driving force of a passionately held faith–once briefly lost and then more vigorously renewed–could have enabled her to endure the rigours of her Siberian journey.

Having trained as a nurse at the Tottenham hospital, which was run by Evangelical Deaconesses on strongly religious lines, she was dispatched in 1877 to nurse the Russian wounded in the Russo-Turkish war. It was here that a chance encounter with two Bulgarian lepers hiding in a barn sparked off her lifelong vocation:

My first acquaintance with the ravages of the frightful disease arose during the Russo-Turkish war. Since then, except during the period when I took many backward steps and turned away from Christ–a memory ever fraught with the keenest regret–the main subject of my thoughts has been the wants of the lepers and how to relieve them. The emotions aroused by the sight of two poor, mutilated, and helpless Bulgarians cannot be fully described. Before this time the conviction had taken hold upon me that my mission in life was to minister to those who received the smallest attention and care of all God's creatures. I had seen and heard of disease and suffering

A classic book of travel in the grimmer regions of the East by Mildred Cable and the sisters Evangeline and Francesca French describes their travels across the Gobi desert, still one of the most desolate parts of the world. They crossed and recrossed its wastes five times in 15 years. One of the sisters is seen here (far right, second row) after escaping from Shan-Si where she had journeyed from Kie-Hiu to Ping-Yang-Fu to escape the Boxers and almost certain death.

When Kate Marsden's father died, leaving the family ill-provided for, she trained to be a nurse. On arrival in Moscow, she joined the Princess Shachovsky (right) and three sisters of mercy who were already working amongst the lepers. She was only 30 years old.

enough amongst the poor of my own country and amongst the victims of war. But they were within close reach, at least, of abundant Christian and philanthropic efforts. But the lepers in the far-off uncivilized regions of the world–who cared for them? What medical attention did they receive? What tender ministration from the gentle hand of woman soothed their sufferings? Cut off from their fellow-creatures, avoided, despised, and doomed to a living death–surely these, of all afflicted people, ought to become the object of my mission.

The traumatic memory stayed with her for thirteen years, during which she consolidated her nursing career in England, then fell ill with suspected tuberculosis, but recovered sufficiently to take up the post of Lady Superintendent at Wellington Hospital in New Zealand. She seems to have made a great success of her job until some form of mental illness intervened, and perhaps the loss of faith alluded to in the preceding extract from her writing. It may have been some sort of dramatic compensation for her lapse that made her determine on her mission with lepers. Accordingly in 1890 she sought the help of Queen Victoria, in the form of an introduction to the Empress of Russia, who was impressed by 'the highly Christian and sincerely philanthropic significance' of the proposed journey to Siberia and wrote her a letter which urged all authorities to co-operate with her in her inspection of lepers' hospitals. The sanction most valued by Kate, however, was a message from 'that ideal servant of the sick and suffering, dear to every Englishwoman':

> May the Father Almighty, Omniscient, who is Infinite Love, be your Guide and your Help in the prayer of, Yours sincerely,
>
> *Florence Nightingale*

In Moscow to prepare for their departure for Siberia, Kate and her companion Miss Field included, among their more obvious supplies of sardines, biscuits, bread and tea, 40 lbs of plum pudding, rationalizing that 'this delicious compound would certainly "keep" in cold weather, as all housewives know'. They also took two dozen boxes of oil wicks and were then told they had enough to last for ten years. Weighed down with provisions and bundled in layers of protective clothing including Jaeger undergarments (to which, together with abstinence, Kate later attributed her survival), ulsters, sheepskins, reindeer skins, felt boots, fur-lined hats, shawls and rugs, they had some difficulty in getting started at all.

> Three muscular policemen attempted to lift me gently into the sledge; but their combined strength was futile under the load. So they had to set me on the ground again. Then I attempted, in a kind of majestic, contemptuous way to mount

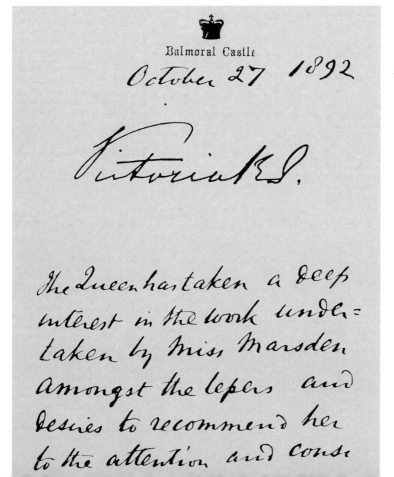

One of Queen Victoria's aides wrote sympathetically to Miss Marsden about her work amongst the lepers, which had already attracted support from the aristocracy of Russia.

Balmoral Castle

October 27 1892

Victoria R.I.

The Queen has taken a deep interest in the work undertaken by Miss Marsden amongst the lepers and desires to recommend her to the attention and conse

without assistance; but, alas! my knees would not bend. My pride had to succumb; I was helpless. Two policemen came and essayed another manoeuvre. They took me by the arms and then, at their signal, I made one desperate, frantic effort, and I was in . . .

My friend, Miss Field, underwent an ordeal somewhat similar to that which I had endured; the driver and the soldier took their seats; and then we were off.

In her autobiographical account of the journey, Kate Marsden slyly postulates the incredible notion that her readers might undertake a similar journey, and draws them into a subjective consideration of all the discomforts she endured:

Our experience of sledging along a road terribly broken up, owing to the immense traffic and almost endless string of sledges carrying heavy loads of goods to the annual Siberian fair, held in February, will be repeated in your case, dear reader, if you ever undertake a similar journey to Siberia at a corresponding period. Bump, jolt, bump, jolt–over huge frozen lumps of snow and into holes, and up and down those dreadful waves and furrows, made by the traffic–such is the stimulating motion you will have to submit to for a few thousand miles. Your head seems to belong to every part of the sledge; it is first bumped against the top; then the conveyance gives a lurch, and you get an unexpected knock against the side; then you cross one of the ruts, and, first, you are thrown violently forward against the driver, and, second, you just as quickly rebound. This sort of motion is all very well for a few miles; but after a time it gets too monotonously trying. You ache from head to foot; you are bruised all over; your poor brain throbs until you give way to a kind of hysterical outcry; your headgear gets displaced; your temper, naturally, becomes slightly ruffled, and you are ready to gasp, from so frequently clutching at the sides to save yourself.

When the jolting stopped, the party put up for the night at 'hotels' which were hot, foetid shacks with no service. Their food consisted of their own supplies–those which had not bounced out of the sledge or been flung to the wolves whose eyes gleamed menacingly in the forest. Kate's bed was a grubby sheepskin laid on the floor, and again invoking the reader's reluctant participation she explains: '. . . but don't imagine you have sole possession of it. One glance around the walls at the numbers of moving specks upon them of different sizes and families will at once dispel that illusion.'

In 1891 no permanent shelter existed for lepers–they lived as outcasts in lonely parts of the forest or marshes, doomed to a living death. Kate's quest to find them and make a report on their predicament took her further and further from any form

MISSIONARIES

of civilization. Yakutsk was, in addition, the coldest place in
the world–92 degrees below freezing for eight months a year,
the ground frozen to a depth of 30 feet. In the brief summer
the heat and mosquitoes were unendurable. Kate managed to
rise above the loss of her companion Miss Field, whose ill-health
forced her to drop out; she managed to manipulate her party
with only twelve words of Russian; but those mosquitoes were
a frightful and recurring tribulation:

> The next day we started early, and our torments from
> mosquitoes began. They literally swarmed around us, and,
> in spite of gloves and a special arrangement for the head and
> shoulders, my hands, wrists and face become swollen to
> alarming dimensions. These pests seemed to besiege every
> crevice where they could contrive to squeeze their bodies in.
> It was impossible to do much in trying to drive them off, for
> I dared not let go the reins, which, by the way, were very
> primitive of their kind and very hard–made of horses' tails–
> and, before long, wore out my gloves and blistered my hands.

Through it all the comparison of her own plight with the lepers'
was what sustained her: 'But those lepers–they suffered far more
than I suffered, and that was the one thought, added to the
strength which God supplied, that kept me from collapsing
entirely.'

Altogether Kate visited lepers in thirteen different places
until she was too ill to go further. Her researches revealed unim-
aginable horrors. The outcasts lived in tiny overcrowded huts,
often sharing their premises with a cow, sleeping on benches
or bare earth. They were almost naked in sub-zero temperatures. They had no weapons, a dog was their only defence
against wolves and bears. They had to drag their mutilated
bodies across the snow to fetch food left at a distance by terrified
relatives. If they had any strength left they made a fire, if not,
they remained in the cold. When they died the bodies remained
in the hut with the others, or were dragged into the snow to
be left for wild animals. Kate omitted nothing from her report
to the authorities.

> In some places the yourtas are small, even for two people;
> but we found as many as eight and ten people in them. The
> dirt, the frightful odour from the lepers, the absence of any
> sanitary place, their food, chiefly consisting of fish, and often
> rotten fish, butter and grease that they drink, and bark of
> trees, and their disgusting clothes, will hardly give you an
> idea of the miserable conditions under which they barely
> exist. It is true what Father John of Viluisk says, that in all
> the world you will not find people in a more lost condition
> than they are. The terror the Yakuts have of this disease is
> remarkable; nothing in the world would make them touch
> or go near them. Be it father, mother, or child, they are torn

MISSIONARIES

away from their family, and condemned to live alone to the
end of their life.

She had seen enough to galvanize any government into action,
and by this time her battered frame refused to take any more
punishment. It is extraordinary to think that this account of
her return journey was written by a valetudinarian who a few
months earlier had never even ridden a horse:

> Having resumed our journey through the forest, I became
> so ill after a few miles that we had to halt. I doubt if any
> of my readers have ever experienced such utter exhaustion
> of both mind and body; my hands literally refused to hold
> the reins. There lay the reins; I knew they had to be held,
> but I was totally incapable of communicating any power to
> my hands. Added to this, I was suffering acute pain from
> an interior abscess, which the constant riding had formed.

She never fully recovered her health, but her findings were
acknowledged and brought results in Russia. In England she
was presented to Queen Victoria and made a Fellow of the
Royal Geographical Society. Dorothy Middleton, her biographer, discovered the most gratifying accolade for the expedition
when she corresponded with Professor N. Torsnev, a Soviet
authority on leprosy. A hospital was opened at Viluisk in 1897,
reaching maximum admission by 1902. Now the hospital is
closed, the spread of the disease having been brought under
control.

Inaccessibility was no deterrent to the woman missionary. In
1899 a missionary from India named William Carey was travelling through Yatung in Tibet with the private secretary to
Bishop Welldon and both were finding it an exotic experience:
'It was a new, not to say exhilarating sensation to find ourselves
... roaming about in the Forbidden Land and being scowled
back with the usual cutthroat gestures.' But forty-year-old Miss
Annie Taylor had preceded them there, and far from being
'scowled back' she had lived there for four years, the only missionary who was tolerated actually *in* Tibet. She traded there
in cloth, sweetmeats and ornaments as well as in Christian souls.
William Carey was keen to visit her, for she was widely famed
for her remarkable Tibetan journey made in 1892–3. Starting
from north China near the Great Wall, Miss Taylor had entered
Tibet, penetrated almost to Lhasa, and returned by another
route, accompanied by a Tibetan youth named Pontso who was
her convert. Carey described his meeting with her in his *Travel
and Adventure in Tibet*:

> We found her a strange complexity of daring, devotion, and
> diplomacy. I do not wonder that the government regarded
> her as a thorn in its side. We listened for hours as she chatted
> over the teacups in her little box of a room, slowly taking

in the perspective of the story with all the advantage of a natural background and local colour. This much was clear, that she had consecrated her life without stint to the service of Jesus Christ, on behalf of Tibet, and had succeeded in bringing the claims of that hard field very closely home to the Christian heart.

The only account of her adventures so far published was a disappointing booklet called *Pioneering in Tibet* which rather meagrely sketched her great journey. Naturally, the inquisitive Carey enquired after the existence of a journal.

> Miss Taylor opened a drawer and took out a black notebook with faded red edges, much besmeared and soiled with dirt and wet.
> 'This,' she said, 'is my diary. I carried it in my dress all the way to Nag-chu-ka and back, and wrote in it every day. But the writing is so illegible that I doubt if anybody could read it. I have the greatest difficulty in reading it myself. There are parts which I cannot make out at all.'

Carey left without the diary, feeling 'Delicacy forbade that a stranger should pry into that private record,' but when he began to write his missionary monograph on Tibet Annie Taylor consented to send it to him. In due course it arrived, smelling strongly Tibetan, having been packed with butter, boar-skins, dried mutton and yaks' tails. It appeared as the second half of his book, with very little editing: 'no sentence has been touched that could be left and . . . the story as it is now published is the story as it was pencilled down under the freezing skies and over the bleak passes of wild Tibet.' There is no comparison to be made between Annie Taylor's mundane jottings, never intended for publication, and the considered literacy of Kate Marsden. One gets no feeling from the diary of the awesome country through which she struggled, the first foreign woman ever to penetrate so far into Tibet.

> *Feb. 21.* This valley is the best for scenery I have seen. It is narrow with high walls. Rock, grass and bush make up the picture. The river is deep and very swift. Every now and then the water breaks through the thick ice.

But even her laconic reportage cannot diminish the scale of her faith and tenacity: 'God will take care of us . . . He has sent me on this journey and I am his little woman. He will protect me.' And this spare account of an attack by brigands stimulates the imagination quite as much as anything more elaborate:

> By this time robbers were seen on the tops of the hills all round, and they were closing in upon us. There was nothing to do but to stand still. Then they fired on us from all sides.

Men and horses fell down dead or wounded. Bullets were flying. There was hardly a sound to be heard except the guns and the cries of fear from the Lhasa women.

On a less dramatic level, there were daily difficulties to contend with. Annie was sick after eating local mushrooms–'Tibetan food and my digestive apparatus not being accustomed to each other. They will get better on further acquaintance.' Soon her digestion was cast-iron and her chief worry was stopping crows stealing meat off the ponies' backs so that the party was not deprived of a supper of fried mutton and barley-flour, 'which we all enjoy, hunger being the best sauce'. She may have shared Kate Marsden's fixation about Christmas pudding, for she begged some suet, a few currants, some black sugar and a little flour to make one for Christmas. It was consumed at altitude (the normally uncomplaining Annie revealed she was suffering from palpitations) and was perhaps not a complete culinary triumph:

> Although the pudding was boiled for two hours it was not warm in the middle. This is a strange climate. We drink our tea at boiling point ladling it out of the pan with our wooden bowls and find it not at all too hot. If we do not drink it at once it gets covered with ice. We are very very cold at night and in the early morning.

But Annie was not critical: 'A nice Christmas day, the sun shining brightly. I had fellowship in spirit with friends all over the world. Quite safe here with Jesus.'

Her resolve was stronger than any of her companions. Even her faithful servant Pontso despaired when their horses began to die under them.

> *Nov. 14.* My poor old red horse . . . could go no further and just lay down and died.
> *Nov. 15.* Over another pass. We had just descended when my little white pony lay down under me.
> *Nov. 20.* I have got so thin and am so exhausted that it looks as if I could not go on without a good horse. God will provide one for me–Pontso has been crying today.

But Pontso's commitment to the expedition was never in question for he was an ardent convert to Christianity. Penting, another Tibetan, seemed loyal enough, if lacking in stamina. The major burden to the expedition was the behaviour of the Chinese Noga, whose dishonest activities crop up like a *leitmotif* throughout the diary. Within a fortnight of setting off Annie records that he was wearing one of her flannel jackets:

> *September 18.* I asked Noga in the morning to give me the jacket, as Pontso and I had no more clothing, and charged

Annie Taylor, disguised as a Tibetan, was allowed to live in Tibet for over four years, and almost reached Lhasa. The brave woman was turned back only three days short of the city. She finally settled on the border of Sikkim and Tibet, where she distributed Christian tracts to Tibetan traders, and became a local character known as anni, *a Tibetan word for 'aunt'.*

79

While at Darjeeling on the Sikkim–Bhutan border, Annie Taylor heard a voice say, 'Go to China'. She did so, taking Pontso, her faithful young servant. He was an ardent convert and believed like her that it would be possible to convert the Tibetans to Christianity.

him with taking the two fur gowns. He got into a rage; and, coming over to where I was lying down, attempted to strike me. Pontso and the servant prevented him; and I ran out, going into one of the Mongol tents for refuge. The people were most kind, giving me milk to drink. I sent for the lama to help me. He came and spoke to Noga, and another of the Mongols took my part. They put up my tent for me, and I said that I must return to Tau-chau, as I could not go on with such a man. All day long they talked, but it was to no purpose. Noga quarrelled with the lama. The lama was most kind.
September 19. Pontso kept guard over me.

After two months of thefts, confrontations and unpleasantness the whole party was threatened by him:

Nov. 6. Noga says he will not go into Lhasa with me, but choose a round-about way, and meet me somewhere on the other side. May the Lord preserve us from all his wickedness!
November 7. Noga quarrelled with his wife, and she came to me in tears. He said he would tell the authorities at Lhasa that she had brought an Englishwoman there from China, and that they would give him a lot of money for the information, and punish her, while he would be safe, as he is Chinese. The Lord will take care of us, I do not fear.

Soon after this Pontso concluded that the only solution was to kill Noga, or be killed himself for leading Annie Taylor to the Forbidden City of Lhasa. Predictably, Annie would not consent to the taking of life and told him that God would save them. Poor Pontso was covering his options by then, for he had been to the temple and worshipped the idols with Penting, causing Annie much pain by his lapse. On their final approach to Lhasa, Noga tried to incite the people to waylay and kill Annie, saying that she was carrying gold and jewels–and then, unaccountably, he and his wife left the expedition. The diary is as laconic as ever: 'We had the pleasure at midday of seeing Noga and his wife depart . . . I must say I have no wish ever to see them again.' But Noga carried out his threat of revealing that an English-woman was on her way.

She was arrested and brought before a military chief who was rather daunted by her firmness and passed her on to a senior official some miles away. An escort of thirty soldiers accompanied her, provoking the comment, 'I truly felt proud of my country when it took so many to keep one woman from running away.' Annie insisted on stopping to make the tea–'I have no intention of being a regular prisoner; so I act just as usual.' The civil chief took down a statement from her and asked her father's name and occupation. Annie understood the Tibetan bureaucratic mentality very well: 'As he is the head of his firm, I said he was a chief. My brother and brother-in-law both being in the Indian Civil Service I was able to say that they were chiefs too.' This declaration of pedigree may have accounted in some measure for the procession of chiefs who then inter-rogated her, reducing Pontso to a state of tearful terror. Nothing intimidated Annie, who continued to insist that Noga be dealt with, who protected Pontso and demanded supplies, horses and safe conduct out of Tibet–'I had to be very firm as our lives seemed to rest on my taking a firm stand.' She threatened to report the magistrate 'to the chief of our country', a ruse which worked very well for he was 'much more civil after this', and her indomitability won her some of her possessions back from Noga, a horse, a tent, provisions and an escort of ten soldiers.

The journey out of Tibet in many ways was worse than the journey in. The soldiers abandoned them after a few days and they proceeded alone. There were objections from Pontso and Penting that they would be attacked, 'but it was clear that if we delayed long on the road we should be frozen'. It was bitterly cold and Annie's health began to deteriorate: 'I cannot walk for more than a few yards, but I can stick on the saddle.' First Penting's horse and then Pontso's died of cold and exhaustion. Pontso covered his with a blanket and walked away with his eyes full of tears. At last they came to the town of Jyekundo on 21 February, in time for Chinese New Year, and took lodg-ings with a relation of Penting's–'They made a place for me on a raised bed of mud,' wrote Annie, with apparent gratitude. It sooned emerged that many of Annie's possessions were missing, stolen by the previously irreproachable Penting, including her hot-water bottle and her English clothes, neither of which could have been of any possible use to him. Annie was extremely annoyed ('It is too bad of him not to give them up') but she had not the heart to dismiss him. It was a relief when his chief refused Penting permission to travel on with her, and she behaved in a truly magnanimous fashion by giving him two horses, the tent, a sheepskin gown and ten rupees in silver. For once it was Penting's turn to burst into tears.

Mildred Cable waiting for her camel en route to the Gobi Desert.

Annie Taylor reluctantly handed over her diary to her biographer, Carey, who overcame his feeling that 'Delicacy forbade that a stranger should pry'.

CHAPTER 4

HUNTRESSES

Smart shooting clothes were worn by some huntresses such as this outfit called a Costume d'Ecosse, *designed about 1875.*

In 1882 Queen Victoria expressed a view held by many when she wrote in a letter to her daughter Princess Victoria that it was acceptable for a woman to be a spectator, but only fast women shot. Mary Kingsley (1862–1900), pioneer of anthropological work in Africa, agreed with her. But although Mary was possessed of a Victorian sense of dress and decorum, she was blessed with a wildly unconventional mind. So, though pacifist by inclination, she was completely matter-of-fact about the possibility of bloodshed between her and the Fans, the primitive tribe with whom she travelled in 1896:

> We knew we should have killed each other if sufficient inducement were offered, and so we took a certain amount of care that the inducement should not arise.

When inducement did, in the form of a crocodile while she was 'fooling about in mangrove swamps', her novel method of dealing with it was to fetch it 'a clip on the snout with a paddle'. Even a leopard about to spring induced no volley of shots from her, but rather a volley of wooden stools and a cooking pot which seem to have subdued it totally. She remarked subsequently:

> I have never hunted a leopard intentionally; I am habitually kind to animals and besides I do not think it is ladylike to go shooting things with a gun.

As late as 1917 Lord Warwick, then aged seventy, said, 'I have met ladies who shoot and I have come to the conclusion, being no longer young and a staunch Conservative, that I would prefer them not to.'

Huntresses who killed men seemed able to earn the approval that eluded huntresses of game. In the mid-nineteenth century Lady Jane Digby, whose globe-trotting, four marriages and scandalously complex love-life brought her plenty of contemporary opprobrium, was much admired by Orientalists Isobel and Richard Burton and Anne and Wilfrid Blunt for her vigorous involvement in Syrian inter-tribal skirmishes. By this time the wife of Sheik Medjuel El Mezrab, she was of sufficient status to ride a horse–the other Bedouin women only rated camels–and galloped alongside her adopted people. She paid for their guns and energetically joined their reprisals against any who invaded their area or stole their cattle. By 1855 she rode into battle for three weeks against an enemy led by Bolo Pasha to avenge a theft which included her favourite mare. A Boadicean entry in her diary reads:

> Cannon and musketry was heard in the morning and . . . Hassam Bey had indeed attacked our camp with Ibn Mershid and after pouring a volley of balls into our tents had carried off all our camels, but, thank God, had killed none of our men.

But English game huntresses, whether they killed for the pot, for pleasure or for self-protection had to contend well into the 1920s with notions of what was 'ladylike'. European women shot more regularly: the wayward Empress Eugénie is shown in an engraving surrounded by a sea of dead birds, and Austrian, German and French shooting parties often included women. 'Abroad' was as usual the haven for those with unconventional ambitions, and it was the Empire that bred a race of huntresses. The big-game shoot was the playtime of the empire-builders: men and women sported together in a welter of congenial bloodletting. Nowadays their memoirs have to contend with modern notions of conservation, although there seems to be a curious link between hunting and love of nature. In some cases this comes across the years as mere fashionable sentimentality, such as Agnes Herbert's unthinking rhapsodies in her book *Two Dianas in Somaliland*: ''Twas like a scene from Shakespeare's woodlands' precedes a gory description of the decapitation and skinning of a hyena. Mrs WW Baillie, shooting in Chamba in the Himalayas in the 1920s, coos over a patch of violets before embarking on a catalogue of death that included hart, tiger, red bear, brown bear and bison. But many huntresses such as Karen Blixen were passionate and knowledgeable naturalists. Some like Lady Curzon and Elspeth Huxley arrived at conservationist enlightenment after witnessing years of indiscriminate bloodshed.

Perhaps the least appealing period was when trophy-hunting was the mania and skulls and skins the *sine qua non* of colonial interior decoration. Jane Duncan, who herself never carried a gun, was a wry observer of 'lady shooters' in her book *A Summer Ride in Tibet* (1906). She tells us how many a huntress got palmed off with horns that were not the spoil of her own gun: she knew of a Kashmir *shikhari* (hunter) who had been taking

The Princess Helene d'Orleans toured Africa in 1910 and here is a typical hunter's picture of her with a hippo she shot at Buzi, then in Portuguese East Africa. Suspiciously, the two Dianas had no such pictures taken of themselves in flagrante *and it may be wondered if their books are all they seem.*

The Empress Eugénie shooting pheasants in the Bois de Marly, Paris. As well as being an active sportwoman she also opened the world of travel to women when she formally opened the Suez Canal.

the same ibex head up country for six years. Jane Duncan crossed and recrossed the dizzying Chang Lar pass in Western Tibet
aged fifty-six, shrugging off 17,676 feet of altitude as a joke, but
she was obviously surprised by the intrepidity of the lady
trophy-hunter she met at Sonamarg:

> She had been up to Zoji La by herself with a *shikhari* and
> two or three other servants and had shot a black bear, a red
> bear (worth 20 black bears) and two ibex, and then she was
> walking fourteen miles down the valley where she had been
> told there was a leopard . . . . she was going to sit up in a
> tree to watch for (it); she would be securely tied to her perch
> in case of falling asleep.

Trophies were a subversion of the chase with the opportunities
they provided for unscrupulousness, deception and competitive-
ness. Mary Kingsley manifests her customary dryness on the
subject:

> For the benefit of sporting readers whose interest may have
> been excited by the mention of big game, I may remark that
> the largest leopard skin I ever measured myself was, tail
> included, 9 ft 7 ins. It was a dried skin and every man who
> saw it said 'it was the largest skin he had ever seen, except
> one he had seen somewhere else'.

Like other hunters, the Curzons used a Machán *or* Shikar Ladder. *The suppliers of sporting gear sold a portable version which was only 'two coolies' load'. It was fitted with a revolving seat so that the shooter did not have to have eyes in the back of her head.*

'With my last barrel I fired,' is the caption on this picture from the book, A Sportswoman in India. *Her* Machán *is rather elementary which adds to the impression of 'derring do'.*

Another, more beneficial side-effect of game hunting was the relationship formed between the native *shikhari* and the white hunter–the bond of the chase was an equalizing one. Lady Curzon took a keen interest in her husband's shooting expeditions when they travelled together as Viceroy and Vicereine of India, but the fate of their *shikhari* caused her enthusiasm to wane. Two tiger shoots were arranged by the Nizam in April 1902 in Hyderabad. The first was amusingly disastrous. Mary Curzon was up a tree in a *machan* (a small railed platform from which to observe), her husband George with his gun and cartridges beside her. She described the scene:

> .... an old *shikhari* (native hunter) stands on the ladder and usually two or three orderlies perch in neighbouring trees. We had just got in the *machan*, George was loading, Captain Wigram and Major Afzal-ud-daula and a group of servants were standing on the ground, when without warning and with a bold roar out bounded a tiger forty yards away. No group of men ever made such time as the group under the tree. Some climbed the ladder, others trees, and Captain Wigram and Major Afzal-ud-daula ran for their lives and clambered up the elephants by the tails! George, quite unprepared, pulled frantically at his rifle, which was at 'safety' and not cocked, and by the time he got it to go off the tiger was a hundred yards away, bellowing and bounding and scattering humanity and getting clean away. The tiger could not have been fifty yards away while we were under our *machan*, and it would have been a great spectacle if he had met us as we walked through the jungle. We were miserable at our loss of the tiger, but such wild tales were told of hairbreadth escapes that we could only laugh thankfully at the successful stampede of the beautiful Staff pursued by tiger.

A week later the hunting anecdotes took a much blacker form:

> Wednesday (9 April) news came of a tiger 8 miles away ... As the beat got near a big angry tiger dashed out, but was too hidden in the rocks to aim at; so he only bounded about roaring, and then returned to his cave. Then a furious tom-toming and shouting by beaters began, and fuses were thrown among the rocks to dislodge him; and we advanced on our elephants to get a nearer shot, the *shikhari* thinking the tiger was sulking. Still nothing happened, and several *shikaries* boldly descended from the elephants to direct the beat, and the line of guns closed up. Captain Wigram, horrified to see men on the ground while a tiger was known to be within a few yards, shouted to the men to get back in the trees and to their elephants, but, alas! too late, as with a roar the tiger dashed out in hot pursuit of a flying *shikhari*. Captain Wigram fired as it came on, but the beast was too near the man to

aim, and with a wild leap the tiger bounded on the man, and as he and the man went down I saw the great jaws close on the back of the man's head. I said to George, 'The tiger has killed a man,' but he had not seen it and said 'I think you are mistaken.' In the meantime four seconds were passing while both man and beast were in sickening silence behind a rock. Then back came the tiger, slowly *trotting*; again Captain Wigram shot, and although the shot killed, the tiger got back to his cave. Then I said to George, 'Now we must go on', so I turned to our *shikhari* to ask him to tell the mahout to go ahead to the left; but I saw a blank space where the old man had been, so I said 'Why, our old *shikhari* has got down. What can he have been dreaming of as we are alone?' With great difficulty we got the mahout to move the elephant to where I thought the wounded man was. By this time everything was roar and confusion, elephants coming up on all sides and no one knowing what had happened. Slowly we lurched forward round the rocks, and there lay a man stone dead, and I said to George, 'It is our own dear old *shikhari*, and I saw him killed.' I had not dreamt who it was, as in the second leap of the tiger I only saw a man in the *shikhari*'s brown uniform and little knew our *shikhari* had left the howdah. A shout came from the rocks that the tiger was dead, so Dr Armstrong and Captain Wigram bounded down, and I threw them ice which I had in the howdah, but the man was dead, and his head half gone from the awful maul of the tiger. The shock of the accident was awful, and only Captain Wigram and I had seen the whole thing happen. The poor old man was put on an elephant's ladder, covered with the folds of his turban, and borne back solemnly through the scorching forest. He was a most fearless old veteran and had once before been mauled by a tiger, and had proudly shown us the scars on his head. He was the Nizam's old *shikhari*, and so the gloom was very deep that this fine old hunter should lose his life by an act of folly . . .

Next day proved a blank day, and I went to Hyderabad, as Mrs Barr had arranged a Purdah party for me before the return of the male members of the party, and I was glad to go as the accident had sickened me for wild animals.

Viceregal shooting parties were splendid affairs that were a form of propaganda; as much to do with demonstrating the power of British rule as with sport. A visit from Viceregal guests could put a great strain on those accustomed to taking their pleasures more simply. Olive Smythies was the wife of a Forest Officer whose job took him to the remotest parts of the Indian jungle. She accompanied him in the saddle and under canvas to unknown places where they encountered all sorts of wild life. They spent at least seven months of the year in the great Terai forests away from their hill station of Naini Tal. But since their period in India spanned the peak of the British presence, from the coronation of George V as Emperor at Delhi in 1911, to the exodus of the British in 1947, they had to cope occasionally with the formal demands of a shoot for distinguished guests, as Olive describes in her book *Tiger Lady*:

> The party arrived at the jungle station, twenty miles from our shooting block, direct from Viceroy House, New Delhi. So far, they had only seen India in a blaze of oriental splendour, and had been accustomed to the pomp and glory that pertains to Viceregal Lodge and ruling Princes. My husband hired two cars and a lorry, which he thought ample for a shooting party of five, but as the overladen train disgorged its contents, he realised something desperate would have to be done. The luggage in itself was overwhelming.
>
> He started by hiring a warehouse! The Countess and the Baroness had brought between them eighteen wardrobe trunks, which were immediately dumped into the warehouse. They had also brought along two European valets and a maid, who could not likewise be dumped but for whose accommodation we were totally unprepared.
>
> In India travellers always take about with them their roll of bedding, blankets, sheets, pillows, etc., except (as we soon discovered) Counts and Barons. So we had to dive into the bazaar and buy up the complete stock of Indian quilts and some lumpy cushions. Towels were also non-existent, so we added to our purchases a few yards of white dhotis (with which Indians wrap their nether parts).

There is an echo of Mary Kingsley's sardonic reaction to trophy-mania in Olive Smythies's explanation to her guests:

> Having studied lists of records of 11- and 12-foot tigers, our guests seemed rather disappointed at the mere 9- and 10-foot samples we bagged. We had to explain that a tiger over 10 feet was quite exceptional, one over $10\frac{1}{2}$ feet was phenomenal, and one of 12 feet was a —— lie. The biggest tiger I ever saw shot was 10 feet 3 inches and I have seen many shot in the United Provinces. We also mentioned the old story of the alleged 12-foot tigers being measured with special steel tapes beautifully graduated in feet and inches and even quarter-inches, but (unknown to the distinguished guest) each 'inch' measuring only 5/6ths of an inch, so that automatically a 10-foot tiger is promoted to 12 feet.

Olive herself had taken up shooting as an eighteen-year-old bride newly arrived in India, to occupy the time when her husband Evelyn was away inspecting the forests–'I was not keen on knitting and embroidery work and there would be few books to read. *Shikhar* would thus afford a welcome relief from monotony'. Once she had executed her first mountain goat, half-way down a precipice, her devotion to her new past-time excluded the possibility of boredom. This is her account of a 'jolly' Christmas shoot:

> Our party consisted of ten, and we spent the days wandering through the jungle or roaming the grassy plains, shooting at whatever game we saw. In the forests we hoped to find *sambar* (large deer), while in the grass our prey was swamp deer, partridges and peafowl. At midday we climbed from the elephants to enjoy a sumptuous lunch which had been carried by a special elephant under the care of two table servants.

> One day we passed some wild plum bushes where a party of five bears were having a feast. Three of these we shot, but a fourth bear, wounded and mad with rage, attacked Kathleen, the elephant upon which my husband and I were riding. Kathleen cared little for tigers, and had never been known to fear anything. The mad, charging bear, however, was too much for her. She fled.

The caption for this picture of Olive Smythies aims to put a light touch to a serious subject. It reads 'The tiger that climbed a tree, the rifle he bit, the Machán *he scratched, and the lady he nearly killed'.*

It is a terrifying experience to be on the back of a stampeding elephant. I clung to my husband, who in turn clung to the *mahawat*, who was beating Kathleen on the head with his iron prong as hard as he could. Finally he managed to stop her, much to our relief, before she reached some thick jungle. Had the elephant plunged into it, we should soon have been swept from her back by the tangle of tree branches overhead.

In the evening, seated round a huge bonfire of logs and

branches of trees, we had sing-songs or told *shikhar* stories.

More often she hunted informally with her husband and their *shikhari* Jankru Singh, a constant source of encouragement. The birth of a son did not deter her from her sport–she simply took an *ayah* and a cow on the camping expeditions. 'Now I wonder how I dared go off into the wilds with a small baby . . . I had no appreciation of the risks I was taking.' They shot for the pot, for food was none too plentiful. 'We sank to the level of shooting partridges and pheasants on the ground and in trees.' They also killed bears which were ravaging the foodstocks of local villages; like many hunters they were in demand as a form of pest control. In view of her proficiency, it is interesting to read that there was still some male chauvinism concerning which animals it was proper for her to hunt: 'My brother-in-law did not approve of women engaging themselves in big-game shooting, but when he saw how very keen I was to get a tiger . . . he did his best to help me.' His counsel was on no account to fire at the tiger's head, but the animal was so well camouflaged that Olive could see no other part of it, and could not even guess where its heart might be:

> Disregarding all advice, I soon had my sights between the tiger's eyes. I took steady aim, fired, and the tiger fell where it stood shot through the brain. It was a male, measuring 9 feet 6 inches between pegs. The fact that I had been able to take such steady aim was solely due to the skill of the *mahawat* in keeping his elephant still. Incidentally, I had to thank him for spotting the tiger so quickly.

While she found the whole episode thrilling, she also felt regret at killing such a beautiful creature, but her interpretation of her feelings would please neither feminists nor conservationists today: 'I often felt that after a kill. I suppose the only explanation is the illogicality of woman!'

According to Olive, any reticence about killing might be interpreted as cowardice by their impressionable orderlies, and British supremacy thereby dented. In the context of this belief, both she and her husband can be seen as sensitive hunters in this episode of the destruction of 'a young and beautifully marked panther':

> An excited orderly pushed a rifle into my husband's hand, loaded but at safe; I would have much preferred a camera at that moment, however. Frankly I did not want to see the panther shot. It seemed a shame to kill that splendid, unsuspecting brute, but by now my husband had a certain reputation as a hunter to maintain, and if he refrained, our orderlies' untutored minds would regard any hesitation on his part to shoot as funk. Reluctantly, for I could see he shared my own feelings, he fired and killed the panther. We went

The elephant was the normal mode of transport for smart shooting parties like those mounted for Mrs Olive Smythies in the reign of George V. Here she is on a typical tour. Picture books of the period frequently illustrate the elephants being attacked by a leaping tiger, but it is doubtful if this happened as often as the artists believed.

down and dragged the animal into the shade of some thick shrubs, and then proceeded on our journey up the valley.

Lady Jenkins (1869–1933) heard not a batsqueak of conservation. Her book *Travel in Both Tibets* is an unselfconscious catalogue of slaughter. Just once she refrains from shooting some wild horses, but she is distinctly cross with herself afterwards. Like many huntresses, she is sentimental about domestic animals ('my poor pony became quite breathless'), while dispatching a wild one in the next sentence; in this case a gazelle. There is a positive schizophrenia in her remark: 'There were a great many marmots–dear little furry beasts–all about this country, but they always escaped before I could get a shot at them.'

Although Lady Jenkins was a Somaliland veteran of five tigers, she seemed an unlikely huntress to her Tibetan guide, who was amazed that the Ladysahib, 'looking like a town lady and not a *shikhari*, and being horribly weak and thin, could be so strong and walk so well'. A far cry from the Viceregal shooting-party guests, she believed in travelling light and managed without everything except food, clothes and ammunition. She shrugged off altitude problems as 'a foolish question of nerve which can soon be overcome'. But even she, struggling through the featureless and desolate Lungnak La Pass confesses to 'loneliness and misery', wishing she had an English-speaking companion, or a book, or even a candlestub to read by.

It was not unusual for ladies to illustrate their books with pictures of themselves in court dress, as authoress Diana did in her first book. But the other 20 photographs in the book nowhere record her actual presence in Somaliland, nor that of her companion, the other Diana, so perhaps they were never there?

Between shots and the lists of her victims, there is some charmingly fresh observation in her account of her expedition, like the description of the waters of Pagong Lake in Tibet: 'hard, rich blue so deep in tone that I quite expected it to be coloured in the little wooden teacups I used for holding my painting water'. Her illustrations are original, too, and perhaps both presage her later development as a novelist, the author of the curiously titled *Through Hawsepipe to Cabin Door* (1924). The book was dedicated to the memory of the old sailing ships and those who sailed in them and concerned Billy, a daredevil boy with golden hair and smiling blue eyes ... perhaps the blue of Pagong Lake. Towards the end of her life she lived in the parish of Llangoedmore, near Cardigan and her trophies still hang on the walls of Cardigan Guildhall.

Trophy mania gave rise to a certain amount of skulduggery. Lady Jenkins's authenticity is unquestionable, but there is definitely something peculiar about the claims made by Agnes Herbert in her book *Two Dianas in Somaliland* (1908). (The title is a reference to the goddess of hunting; the two women concerned are the author and her cousin Cicely.) The illustrations of trophies range from rhinoceros and lion skins to koodoo and oryx skulls. Oddly, their shooters are never pictured with them, and one is forced to conclude that they might have been shot by anyone, anywhere. It is intriguing that a volume with a title page advertising *Twenty-five illustrations reproduced from photographs*

The gun has clearly been superimposed upon the picture of the dead lion, an example of the strange way in which the photographers in the book do not add to the Dianas' credibility.

Clarence is not an authentic native warrior, although the Dianas clearly intended him to be thought a genuine resident of Somaliland.

(actually there are only 22) should contain not a single picture showing the intrepid pair on their hunting trip. Some of the photographs are clearly doctored or faked. Elsewhere, while the animals in the field are clearly dead ones, the mounted specimens could have been photographed in almost any Edwardian stately home.

While one accepts that huntresses still faced disapproval over the ladylike question as late as 1908, the tone of the *Two Dianas in Somaliland* is amazingly coy on the subject. In fact, the book is so brimming with 'Little Woman' asides that it is hard to suppress a growing conviction that it was really written by a man: 'We planned a sporting trip to Somaliland–very secretly and to ourselves, for women hate being laughed at quite as much as men do, and that is very much indeed.' Agnes describes herself as 'by no means a duffer with a rifle' and her cousin Cicely as 'a wonderful shot' but she had to combat her game-hunting uncle's scepticism: 'The fragility of my physique bothered him no end. I assured him . . . that I am . . . a most wiry person.' There is a recurring *Girls' Own* dauntlessness, but is it not usually men who harp on women's intuition? 'As to our courage, we could only trust we had sufficient to carry us through. We felt we had, and with a woman intuition is everything.' All danger is met with a flirtatious flippancy: 'A charge from a maddened bull oryx would be no simple thing. But there came a soft low whinnying noise from the bush: he was off and I was forgotten. *Cherchez la femme*, even in oryx land.'

Lady Jenkins's stoicism makes her seem like a different species when Agnes Herbert complains of the 'appalling heat' and 'frightful discomfort' she endured while choosing her retinue in Berbera. Their caravan consisted of six rough ponies, forty-nine camels, a cook and two assistants, twenty-five camel-men, four grooms, six hunters and a mysterious *shikhari* 'Clarence', who acted as her 'butler' and organized baths in the bush. He is one of several suspicious-looking gentlemen photographed, and to the jaundiced eye seems quite implausible. Agnes stresses he was 'not of Negritic descent' and explains his rather insulting nickname:

> Our would-be henchman's name was unpronounceable, and sounded more like 'Clarence' than anything, so Clarence he remained to the end–a really fine, handsome fellow, not very dark, about the Arab colour, with a mop of dark hair turning slightly grey.

Other fugitives from a game of charades are 'the leader of the Opposition Shoot' who looks as though he may be wearing a false beard, and Ralph, one of his cohorts, who seems unusually suntanned. He struck up a relationship with Cicely which was waspishly observed by Agnes. Defending herself, Cicely said that if someone did not arrange a marriage for her soon, she would be left on the shelf. Agnes countered Sibyl-like, 'One can see a lot from the shelf provided it is high enough,' and when Ralph joined Cicely on a stalking-party speculated darkly, 'I wonder how much stalking they did.'

Almost the only time an authentic note rings out is when Clarence asks Agnes 'if these trophies had some intrinsic value . . . that so many people come at such trouble and danger to themselves to get them? He evidently was much puzzled.' He must have been totally baffled by 'The End of the Great Shikhar' which came when Berbera was in sight again.'

> Clarence helped us pack the trophies in great cases. . . . We counted our gains and found that they included rhino, lion, leopard, hartebeest, dibatag, gerenuk, oryx, aoul, Spekes's gazelle, klip-springer, Pelzeln's gazelle, warthog, hyena, jackal, wolf, ostrich, marabou, dik-dik and one or two other varieties.

The Kenya colonists were not only a byword for their game hunting but for their decadence. In Kenya on Christmas Day 1896, Lord Delamere amused himself by going on a pig-spearing expedition with a Mrs Pease, and having his photograph taken afterwards. On the back of the photograph he wrote, 'all the pigs were speared' (in other words, not shot). We do not know what Mrs Pease's attractions were, apart from her skill with a spear, but one of them may have been that she wore a skirt, and not shorts, of which the young red-headed Delamere did not approve. Shorts had been introduced to Kenya by Lady Idina Gordon which Lady Frances Scott, like Delamere, thought 'very ugly and quite unnecessary' and, she added, they have 'done a lot of harm in this country'. Elspeth Huxley's latest book *Out in the Midday Sun* reveals that Delamere was a woman hunter as well as a pig-sticker, and one to whom the canard applied, 'Are you married or do you live in Kenya?' Of such people Karen Blixen wrote:

> When I observe the situation out here and see how people with the greatest equanimity and social success conduct themselves . . . I am certain the old negative sexual morality has had its day. It may be of course that to a certain extent the country is outside the normal bounds of law and order. There is quite simply nothing that one cannot freely undertake in this direction . . .

Although Karen Blixen admired Lord Delamere, she censured his morality in a broader sense too:

> The upper classes haven't improved in the slightest since the revolution. When they're not *afraid* of the lower classes, they're really completely without shame; the natives can be starving here and dying of starvation . . . and the champagne flows in torrents at their races and so on—Lord Delamere

Ralph, who looks distinctly dark for a genuine hunting companion for a Diana, was thought to have got up to amorous antics stalking.

Mrs Pease was photographed red-handed in Somaliland with the red-headed Lord Delamare (third left) who dislocated his neck while out pig-sticking. One of his other sports was shooting out the lamps in Nairobi's main street. His topee was said to be the largest in Africa as the pioneer was highly susceptible to sun-stroke.

recently held a dinner for 250 people at which they drank 600 bottles and they just do not *see* it; the ladies here are quite capable when they hear that the natives cannot get *posho* [mealies] of asking why they do not eat wheat or rice instead, just like Marie Antoinette . . .

But it took a little longer for Baroness Blixen to become analytical about the morality of hunting. She ran a coffee-plantation in Kenya from 1914–31 and was part of the last wave of colonists that included the young Elspeth Huxley. Both women established a deep permanent involvement with the native population that was far ahead of their time, both responded passionately to the prehistoric call of hunting, and both loved the animals that they shot. Elspeth Huxley acknowledges the enigma that many hunters were great naturalists, and in her book about her childhood, *The Mottled Lizard*, she explains 'the code to make this bloodlust respectable'. Females and young were not to be shot, you must kill 'cleanly' and if any animal was wounded it was your duty to follow it and put it out of its misery. By culling older males–who incidentally made the most magnificent trophies–you would improve the breeding stock. The Boers, who killed indiscriminately for skins and to protect their crops and flocks, the Africans who considered wild animals as a menace to be rid of, and above all, unscrupulous trophy hunters were, to these huntresses, absolutely beyond the

pale. Karen Blixen pours scorn on commercial safaris like that of the rich American Lady Mackenzie, who travelled with seven white men and 200 bearers 'and broke all the rules'. For Baroness Blixen, personal danger was part of the purity of hunting. It was not always so: 'I must humbly apologise to those hunters whose delight in the chase I failed to understand. There is nothing in the world to equal it.'

She was forced to consider the morality of risking one's life for 'fun' when her plantation manager refused to accompany her on a lion hunt. He felt his responsibility for his pregnant wife and small child was too great to risk on a foolhardy expedition: the marauding lion could as well be poisoned. Suppressing her dislike at such an unsporting suggestion, Karen Blixen conceded that married people have a duty to renounce such pleasures. She then issued an invitation to her great love, bachelor Denys Finch-Hatton–'Come now then, and let us go and risk our entirely worthless lives.' The result was a consummate description of 'a real night of *game* in the boma' in which her pleasure in the kill is equalled by her delight in observing the living animal. It seemed entirely fitting that she should have received a letter from an old gun-bearer addressed to *Lioness von Blixen* that began *Honourable Lioness*!

Elspeth Huxley was always more ambivalent about the destruction of beautiful creatures. Some of her happiest hunting days were with an eccentric pack of hounds run by an expatriate Irishman, because their hysteria often enabled the prey to escape. Nearly always regretful after a kill, in her case it does not seem a bizarre step from huntress to conservationist. Taking pictures of her porters holding up her trophies, she 'was no longer sure whether to feel proud or ashamed'. Indeed, it seemed logical to sacrifice a passion for the sport in favour of the wild life she had come to know so well through it.

The Americans Martin and Osa Johnson who hunted in Kenya in the 1920s were very different from the bedhopping sophisticates who earned the colony its reputation for raffish sport of all kinds. They travelled extensively together in pursuit of photographic quarry and killed only to eat, or in self-defence, as Martin explains in his book *Camera Trails in Africa*:

> I am not going as a big-game hunter. There is nothing more disgusting to me than the slaughter of animals for the sake of sport. It is sometimes necessary to kill a gazelle or a zebra for meat. It is occasionally necessary to kill a buffalo or an elephant or a leopard or a lion in order to escape being killed yourself. But on the whole it is safer to live among wild animals than to live in New York. With the exception of the big cats, which are a treacherous lot, few of them will attack unless they are frightened or molested. And I want to live at peace with them.

In practice, Martin shot with film and Osa with bullets, and

The hunt for trophies was part of most people's Indian experience, even the Viceroy's, here seen with the Vicereine about halfway through the Viceregal tour. Before her marriage, Mary Curzon had been Miss Leiter, daughter of a Chicago millionaire, so all this was new to her.

he owed his life to her on more than one occasion. She was a remarkable woman who began life as a singer, married Martin in a whirlwind courtship and became one of the most travelled women of her generation. The dedication of his book speaks volumes about their relationship:

'Civilization is creeping into British East Africa,' wrote the Johnsons and they energetically tried to capture the continent on film before it crept any further.

> To Osa
> The best pal a man ever had
> For fifteen years, she has gone everywhere with me. We have done the Great White Way together. We have sailed together into the cannibal islands of the South Seas. We have explored the Borneo jungle together, and together we have lived among the animals of Africa. Osa has stood by me in every emergency. In Africa, she saved my life from the elephants of Lake Paradise. She has never failed me. And—what counts most—she likes it all!

Without any earlier practice, Osa developed a natural talent for rifle-shooting in the Solomon Islands early in her married life. Within a few days, she began to bring in pigeons, wild goats and fish as a result of her marksmanship. She also showed a facility for picking up local dialects and in later years spoke Malay and Swahili fluently, spending long hours round the campfire listening to tales of hunting and superstition. Their base in East Africa was well away from the flesh-pots, a thousand miles' trek from Nairobi, somewhere near the Abyssinian border. They were deliberately vague about its exact location, for to them it was Paradise, literally and figuratively: '. . . if it were charted it would appear on the maps as Lake Paradise. And I know of no place in all the world that better deserves the name,' wrote Martin. 'Only a few natives and I–and the animals–know exactly where it is. And the animals and I, at least, are not going to tell.'

Osa was indispensable, and not only as a huntress. She helped build their lodge with her own hands; she constructed her own tables and chairs; she planted a vegetable garden and ran a dairy; she organized a laundry and she taught the natives to cook meat and bake bread. 'She was my commissary steward,' said Martin, 'not an easy job five hundred miles from the nearest grocery store.' Osa was an uncannily skilful fisherwoman but there were often setbacks (which she relished), as she describes in her own account *Four Years in Paradise*:

> My first catch, however, was not a fish. Having no sinker with me, I took a bolt and two nuts from one of the motor cars and tied them to my line. The stream was deep and swift and I added weight to clear some reeds beneath my feet. Giving the sinkers a good whirl over my head, I threw them in. There was a terrific grunt as a huge form rose out of the water beneath me. I had hit a hippo clean on the head. He let out a roar, and, thinking he would attack, I beat it up the bank. There I paused to watch the 'submarine' swim off, leaving a great wake behind him–while my boys howled at the joke.
>
> But the most exciting adventure is to be intent on landing a fine large fish after a good fight–to be so intent as to notice nothing about you–then suddenly to look up and find a rhino or buffalo bearing down on you. The boys would yell and there was nothing to do but shoot one's way out or scramble up a tree. I often wondered afterward how I ever managed to get up some of those trees, but under the pressure of saving one's neck wonders can be done.

Her part in their film-making was crucial:

> The feeling that Osa is so accurate a shot means a lot in my camera work. I am usually intent on the focusing and speed of film, and often do not even realise the danger facing us. Osa stands there coolly, gun in hand. If the game is too quiet she wanders forward cautiously and stirs it up. She seems to have no nerves.

Twice she dropped elephants at her husband's feet, and once a lion so close that Martin 'could touch his mane with his toe'. Despite her scruples about killing she found the experience very elating, as Martin relates:

Suddenly Jerramani put his hand on my arm. 'Simba, simba,' he whispered. And there about fifty yards in front of us was a big, black-maned lion, tearing at a zebra he had killed and dragged into the bushes. The lion stood with his back to us, but just as I caught sight of him he turned. For one marvellous second, he stood, fierce and beautiful, his front feet on the zebra he had killed, glaring at us with savage, yellow-green eyes. I watched him, motionless with admiration.

But not Osa. She proved the case of the ayes in the age-old debate, Resolved: That women are more practical than men. Before I knew what she was up to, she seized her .30 from Jerramani and fired at the lion. He had just lifted one foot to turn and go off into the forest, but she brought him down in a heap. He rolled over, whirled in our direction, and (so it seemed to me) made ready for a spring. Then I thought of my camera . . . I sprang to the crank and began to reel off King Lion.

There he crouched big and beautiful. He roared until the thicket shook, baring his great white teeth in a vicious grimace. He tried to spring, but he sank back, powerless, on his haunches, with effort holding himself erect on his forelegs. He roared again. Osa was wild with excitement. She went closer and closer to him, gun in hand, exclaiming over and over: 'Isn't he a beauty! Isn't he a beauty!' He turned his head toward her and snarled, and then with another mighty roar gathered himself painfully together for a spring. 'Look out!' I shouted. But my warning was unnecessary. The King of Beasts had fallen over dead. Osa's bullet had broken his back.

Sometimes their roles were reversed, with Osa on the camera, but on one occasion at least, she had to resort hastily to her rifle. Martin explains apologetically that he 'used to collect a little ivory occasionally', and was stalking a big bull elephant with a fine pair of tusks:

Suddenly the big fellow glanced up and saw me. As I was very close, I fired. I thought I had hit him in a vital spot. Indeed, had Osa been the hunter, the victim would probably have fallen then and there. But somehow I missed the small brain area which the bullet must penetrate to be fatal.

The bull jumped and charged. I ran at top speed toward Osa. She was cranking the camera, getting priceless film as I fled for my life. It may seem to the reader that she was callous in letting the charging elephant come after me and doing nothing about it except take my picture. But her quick eye caught the fact instantly that the elephant was not gaining much.

The great danger to me lay in the possibility that I might stumble. Osa knew this as well as I. More than once she had had to run over rough ground to escape rhinos. Also holding my rifle and glancing over my shoulder made my movements awkward.

She cranked as long as she dared. Then she reached down and grabbed her gun. Under ordinary circumstances I like to see her shoot. She has a natural grace about her whole act of marksmanship that is rare. But this time I was in no mood to appreciate anything but escape.

In a split second she had the rifle to her shoulder and fired. I swerved as the mortally wounded elephant thundered past and fell with a thud that shook us all.

Seeing that the others of the herd were checked and that our danger was over I stepped up to Osa for a word of admiration. She was very pale.

'I–I guess I have to sit down for a minute, Martin,' she said.

I didn't blame her. My own knees felt a little weak.

Osa Johnson was 'the best pal a man ever had', according to her husband. 'She was my commissary steward,' he said, 'not an easy job five hundred miles from the nearest grocery store.' She was not only a good shot, but a keen fisherwoman.

Martin and Osa Johnson saw that there were not many years left to make a record of the wild-life for 'civilisation is creeping into British East Africa and in advance of it are the big-game hunters greedy for trophies and a record bag.' They were pioneers of the wild-life film, which brought with it awareness of endangered species; the preservation of some fast-vanishing breeds is due to them. When one reads Osa's sad description of their final departure from Lake Paradise, it confirms them as the best hunters of them all:

We spent many of these last days at the lake lying on a rock to watch the animals and birds, or walking around its rim as a relief from the work of packing and writing letters and reports.

There in the water one afternoon we saw a great elephant giving himself a bath. He was having a wonderful time all by himself, throwing great streams of water over his body and into the air. As the spray fell it caught the sun and draped a broad rainbow over his bronze back.

Baby giraffe just born – returned by Osa Johnson to its mother and the herd.

I began to cry; it was too beautiful to leave.

'I wonder if my nasturtiums will live by themselves,' I murmured. 'I suppose the birds will carry seeds from the garden and there will be cucumbers and water-melons all over the place.'

'Life is just too short,' Martin went on. 'It's a pity we can't live five hundred years with so much beauty to enjoy and so much work to accomplish.'

As we climbed back up toward camp, his voice trailed on: 'The baboons will live in our houses. They will stuff themselves with tomatoes and the elephants will have a good time in the sweet potatoes. The birds will feast on your flower seeds and on the melons. But only you and I and the animals, Osa, will know where Lake Paradise is. And you and I won't tell.'

Early the next morning, with every porter loaded to capacity and the motor-cars piled high, we started away.

Driving over the rim of the crater, we stopped for a final look.

'It's a Garden of Eden, Martin. I hope it never changes.'

CHAPTER 5

GOVERNESSES

The King and I *was a musical based somewhat loosely on the real-life adventures of Anna Leonowens.*

The real Anna became the King of Siam's trusted confidante, taking over his diplomatic correspondence, including his private letters to Queen Victoria.

The *Quarterly Review* of 1850 describes a governess as 'a being who is our equal in birth, manners and education but our inferior in worldly wealth'. During the nineteenth century it was a status symbol for aristocratic foreign families to acquire one of these genteel paragons to educate their children. The governess was to be found all over the world, even though the standards of tuition were not necessarily very high. *The Child's Guide to Knowledge*, an indispensible schoolroom book of the period, contained such startling useless and irrelevant pieces of information as:

> Q: What is the common maple?
> A: A low tree common in woods and hedges so much valued by the Romans that they gave an extravagant price for it for their tables.
> Q: Are not umbrellas of great antiquity?
> A: Yes; the Greeks, Romans and all Eastern nations used them to keep off the sun; *ombrello* in Italian signifies 'a little shade'.

Of course there were notable academic exceptions, like Anna Leonowens, whose story was dramatized in *Anna and The King of Siam* and later in *The King and I*. She was highly intelligent and in 1862 not only brought order to the schoolroom containing King Mongkut's numerous offspring, but tried to modify the brutality of the tyrannical monarch. She became his trusted confidante, taking over his diplomatic correspondence, including his private letters to Queen Victoria. When she left Siam she wrote two immensely successful books about her experiences: *The English Governess at the Siamese Court* and *Siamese Harem Life*.

Few governesses were as accomplished and articulate, but those who went abroad were perhaps bolder specimens than their stay-at-home sisters, and some have left lively observations

107

of the social scenes in which they found themselves. They travelled primarily to earn a living but to be a successful governess abroad required a curious mixture of qualities: a sense of adventure, a chameleon-like ability to adapt, and a zealous desire to impose 'proper' standards on the charges. Some bright hopes were dashed, like those of the highly intelligent Maria Graham, author of the schoolroom classic *Little Arthur's History of England*, who had to battle against court intrigues when she took charge of the daughter of the Emperor and Empress of Brazil in 1824; the charming French governess Henriette Desportes, whose name was scandalously linked with her employer's in a murder case which titillated the whole of Europe in 1847; vigorous Emmeline Lott who endured, tight-lipped, a life in the harem as governess to the Grand Pasha of Egypt in the early 1860s. Undisputed successes were tactful Anna Bicknell, who was governess to the two daughters of the Grand Master of the Empress Eugénie's household and who observed Court life in the Tuileries in 1852 with a disciplined English eye; the anonymous Miss M—, who always felt her destiny was to be a royal governess and who transformed the life of the lonely young Archduchess Marie of Austria in 1893; and discreet Miss Eagar who took charge of the ill-fated little Grand Duchesses of Russia in 1898, spending six years at the Russian Court.

Maria Graham (1785–1842) was reared as an intellectual: she spent her holidays at the home of her uncle, Sir David Dundas, in Richmond, which he made a centre for scientists, literary men and French émigrés. She was exceptionally well travelled; aged twenty-three she journeyed with her father to India, and subsequently married Captain Thomas Graham RN with whom she sailed the high seas, a privilege then accorded captains' wives. It gave her a taste for adventure and an inner resource which stood her in good stead when her husband died off the coast of Chile in 1822. Tragically alone, she moved on to Brazil, but her *Journal of a Voyage to Brazil*, written in 1824, shows her remarkable resilience:

> Let no one say, that he is too miserable for any comfort to reach him. I am alone, and a widow, and in a foreign land; my health weak, my nerves irritable, and having neither wealth nor rank; forced to receive obligations painful and discordant with my former habits and prejudices, and often meeting with impertinence from those who take advantage of my solitary situation: but I am nevertheless sure that I have more *half-hours*, I dare not say *hours*, of true enjoyment, and fewer days of real misery, than half of those whom the world accounts happy. And I thank God, who gave me the temper to feel grief exquisitely, that he at the same time gave me an equal capacity for joy. And it is a joy to find minds that can understand and communicate with our own; to meet occasionally with persons of similar habits of thinking, and who, when the business of life rests a while, seek recreation

Miss Graham (painted here by Lawrence) became a famous teacher of the young through the medium of her book, Little Arthur's History, *in which she wrote such superfluous information as, 'When Queen Elizabeth ascended the throne . . . she was very pleasant looking' and 'Poor King Edward was taken to Greenwich for a change of air'.*

in the same pursuits. This delight I do oftener enjoy than I could have hoped, so far from cultivated Europe.

She was received by the Emperor and Empress of Brazil, to whom she was immediately drawn:

There was little form and no stiffness. Her Imperial Majesty conversed easily with everybody, only telling us all to speak Portuguese, which of course we did. She talked a good deal to me about English authors, and especially of the Scotch novels, and very kindly helped me in my Portuguese; which, though I now understand, I have few opportunities of speaking to cultivated persons. If I have been pleased with her before, I was charmed with her now. When the Emperor had received the public bodies, he came and led the Empress into the great receiving room, and there, both of them standing on the upper step of the throne, they had their hands kissed by naval, military, and civil officers, and private men; thousands, I should think, thus passed. It was curious, but it pleased me, to see some negro officers take the small white hand of the Empress in their clumsy black hands, and apply their pouting African lips to so delicate a skin; but they looked up to *Nosso Emperador*, and to her, with a reverence that seemed to me a promise of faith *from* them, a bond of kindness *to* them. The Emperor was dressed in a very rich military uniform, the Empress in a white dressed embroidered with gold, a corresponding cap with feathers tipped with green; and her diamonds were superb, her head-tire and ear-rings having in them opals such as I suppose the world does not contain, and the brilliants surrounding the Emperor's picture, which she wears, the largest I have seen.

To her surprise she was put forward as a suitable governess for Their Imperial Majesties' daughter, which astonished her for she was intending to return to England.

> Six months before, indeed, I had said that I was so pleased with the little Princess, that I should like to educate her. This, which I thought no more of at the time, was, like every thing in this gossiping place, told to Sir T. Hardy: he spoke of it to me, and said he had already mentioned it to a friend of mine. I said, that if the Emperor and Empress chose, as a warm climate agreed with me, I should not dislike it; that it required consideration; and that if I could render myself sufficiently agreeable to the Empress, I should ask the appointment of governess to the Princess; and so matters stood when Sir Thomas Hardy sailed for Buenos Ayres. I own that the more I saw of the Imperial family, the more I wished to belong to it; but I was frightened at the thoughts of Rio, by the impertinent behaviour of some of the English, so that I should probably not have proposed the thing myself. It was done, however: the Empress told me to apply to the Emperor. I observed he looked tired with the levée, and begged to be allowed to write to her another day. She said, 'Write if you please, but come and see the Emperor at five o'clock to-morrow.' And so they went out, and I remained marvelling at the chance that had brought me into a situation so unlike any thing I had ever contemplated; and came home to write a letter to Her Imperial Majesty, and to wonder what I should do next.

The matter settled, she returned to London to wind up her affairs, to acquire some teaching aids for her new pupil, and to publish her *Journal*. The latter caused some resentment on her reappearance in Rio from expatriates who were offended by her comments. Their offence-threshold must have been very low if this sort of thing upset them:

> In short, my countrywomen here are a discreet sober set of persons, with not more than a reasonable share of good or bad. They go pretty regularly to church on Sundays, for we have a very pretty Protestant chapel in Rio, served by a respectable clergyman; meet after church to luncheon and gossip: some go afterwards to the opera, others play cards, and some few stay at home, or ride out with their husbands, and instruct themselves and families by reading; and all this

much as it happens in Europe. However, they are all very civil to me; and why should I see faults, or be hurt at the absurd stories they tell of me, because they don't know me? Besides, 'tis no great affront to be called wiser than one is.

The engagement, however, seemed to be a great success. Her Imperial employers and her pupil Doña Maria da Gloria obviously appreciated her, as she wrote to John Murray in September 1824 from the palace in Rio. Rosamond Gotch quotes this letter in her biography of Maria Graham:

The Emperor and Empress received me most kindly. I have a charming apartment of seven little rooms immediately over Her Imperial Majesty. The young Princess and I are already the best friends imaginable, and she has made a bargain that I shall not give her very long lessons ... I am sorry to find that with all my care there are some expressions in my *Brazil* that have offended some of the English here, and I found a regular mutiny against me when I came. However, they are beginning to be ashamed of themselves and are dropping in one by one. I am quite as well pleased not to be on very intimate terms with anybody out of the palace; it removes suspicion of intrigue which is a great advantage, for however free I may be from wishing for secret communications, I shall find few people about a court who will believe in perfect sincerity and openness. However, time will I hope convince them, and, I trust, not alter me.

Despite her balanced evaluation of the problem, Court intrigue was to be her undoing. The Emperor was deeply involved with his brilliant mistress, Doña Domitila de Castro e Mello, and the lonely Empress Leopoldina formed a strong friendship with Maria. Both women were cultivated, sharing a passion for botany. The Court ladies were furiously jealous at this intimacy and contrived to bring about Maria's downfall. Bea Howe, in her definitive book *A Galaxy of Governesses*, describes their campaign as revealed in Maria's unpublished diaries. Maria had been absolved from appearing at many of the boring Court functions, and this, added to her closeness to the Empress, 'swelled into a mighty roar of questions hurled at her turbaned head. Did the Nursery Governess know that she must attend such an important function as the Birthday Court "dressed in the Court Livery of embroidered white satin with a green satin train and white feathers and to stand close by the Throne in case the Royal Child should require her handkerchief?" No, smiled Madam sweetly, she did not. And then, quite calmly she went on to explain that she was not a court servant bound by their laws and she was *not* attending the Birthday Court. Amazed and furious, the Court ladies determined to make Madam pay for what they called her foreign insolence.'
  The Emperor, bored by the complaints, was provoked by the

Princess's chief attendant into finding a solution to all the acrimony. He gave the order that the Imperial Governess should be confined to her quarters outside lesson hours. It was out of the question for the dignified Maria to endure such an insult, and accordingly she offered her resignation. It was devastating for the poor Empress who had come to rely so heavily on her company, undoubtedly it was detrimental to the child, and the Emperor certainly regretted his hasty decision. But Maria's pride would not permit her to reconsider, and on 10 October 1824, only a month after her arrival, she left Brazil for ever. Happily she made a contented life for herself in London, marrying Augustus Wall Callcott RA in 1827 and then establishing herself as the epicentre of the nursery bookshelf for many generations with her best-selling *Little Arthur's History of England*.

If a chameleon-like capacity to blend with her surroundings was a desirable attribute of the governess, Maria Graham did not possess it. Neither did Henriette Desportes (1813–1875), for

The governess was a favourite character in novels of the Regency period–perhaps the most famous being Mrs Weston (née Miss Taylor) in Jane Austen's Emma.

she was a phenomenon among governesses–a notoriously scandalous one. Her remarkable story is told by her great-niece Rachel Field in her book *All This And Heaven Too*. With no close family, Henriette left her native France to take up a post as governess to the only daughter of Sir Thomas Hislop in London. At the end of her engagement her fluent French and English, familiarity with literature and the classics, and talent for painting earned her wonderful references; her strong personality and rapport with the child earned her the affection of the family. It was with regret that they saw her leave to take up a post with the Duc and Duchesse de Praslin at Château Praslin. She knew it would not be easy, for she had heard of a string of predecessors who had not been able to deal with the neurasthenic Duchesse. Unusually for his period, but due to his wife's illness and unbalanced disposition, the Duc supervised his children's lives and education, which brought him into close contact with Henriette. The Duchesse became insanely jealous, accusing her first of alienating her children's affection, then her husband's. The situation became untenable when Henriette appeared in the gossip columns as a rival to the Duchesse. She left their employment with her reputation too damaged to find a new job. The Duc assured her of a reference from his wife which would transform her future opportunities, but while she waited and hoped in near-destitution, she found herself the central figure in a true *cause célèbre*.

The Duchesse was discovered brutally murdered. The Duc was imprisoned at Luxembourg, charged with the murder of his wife, and Henriette was held at the Conciergerie, charged with complicity. Contemporary accounts accused her of a theatrical awareness of herself, a self-conscious posing as she paced her cell. Rachel Field tells us that she did indeed possess dramatic gifts: she was a passionate admirer of the dramatic actress Rachel and read to the children with beautiful expression. With the addition of her quick mind, this flair was instrumental in her acquittal: both the prosecution and defence lawyers were extremely impressed with her demeanour and intelligence in the dock. Any chance Henriette retained of not being permanently imprinted on the public consciousness was removed when the Duc died of self-administered poison while still awaiting trial. She was forced to leave France and endured an uneasy transplantation to America.

But the story has a surprisingly happy ending, for Henriette married the Reverend Henry Field, a well-known American preacher. He was a warm idealist who appreciated her exoticism–though initially her New England relatives did not– and it was an extremely happy marriage until her death in 1875.

Anna Bicknell, who wrote the story of her *Life in The Tuileries Under the Second Empire* in 1895, was by no means colourless, but she was better able to blend in with her chosen family than either of these two predecessors. It was a delicately balanced social world that she entered.

113

Anna's employer, the General Comte de Tascher de la Pagerie, conscientiously opposed the marriage of the Emperor Louis Napoleon to a commoner. However the Emperor made an appeal to his past friendship and loyalty, and finally prevailed on the Comte to run the household of the new Empress. Anna Bicknell therefore came to a family in 1852 whose allegiance to the Empress Eugénie was strong but not completely uncritical, as they tried to mould her from a capricious young gentlewoman into responsible royalty. Anna taught the de Tascher children for nine years, living in the magnificent Palais des Tuileries as part of the royal household under the Second Empire.

To begin with, she was slightly overwhelmed by the grandeur of it all:

> The large handsome dining-room, where the numerous members of the family took their seats, the servants, in and out of livery, the display of plate, and all the ceremony of a formal dinner party, although no strangers were present, made me feel more than ever like a poor little sparrow which had strayed alone into an aviary of tropical birds.

Everyone made her welcome, she was treated kindly, but initially she found her duties oppressive:

> From the moment when I was awakened in the morning till a late hour at night there was not an interval of time to breathe. The two girls being of different ages, the professors, classes, lectures, etc., were also totally different; so my days were spent in rushing out with one, and then rushing back to take the other somewhere else; on foot, in all weathers, which the Duchess considered necessary for the health of my pupils; but, as I had two, the fatigue was doubled. During these lectures, etc., I had to take notes incessantly, and to prepare the work for them. Often I was obliged to dress in ten minutes for a large dinner-party, because some professor had prolonged his lesson to the very last moment. The constant mental strain, added to the physical fatigue, was almost more than I could endure, and my health suffered so severely that I greatly feared the impossibility of continuing such an arduous task. In the evening there were dancing lessons three times a week; one at the English embassy, from which we returned at a late hour, and two others at the Tuileries in the apartments of the Duchesse de Bassano, our next neighbour. On the remaining evenings I frequently accompanied the [Princess] Countess, or the Comtesse Stephanie, to theaters or operas, which, though very agreeable, added considerably to the overwhelming fatigue of the day. As to my own private correspondence, I was obliged to write necessary letters often very late at night, to the great anger of the Duchess, who rightly declared that I was wearing myself out;

but I had no other resource. As time went on, matters happily became more easy, and after the marriage of my eldest pupil with Prince Maximilian von Thurn und Taxis, my task was considerably diminished. The work of the first year, however, was absolutely crushing.

She had, however, the encouraging example of Miss Shaw alongside her in the Tuileries, who was the archetypal English nanny and whose no-nonsense upbringing of the young Prince Imperial earned high commendation from Anna.

The little Prince . . . was accompanied by his English nurse, known as 'Miss Shaw', a perfect specimen of the rules of a nursery among the British aristocracy. She had no easy task in defending the child from the too exuberant endearments of the young ladies present and energetically protested in English that they were 'worrying him and frightening him'.

The Tuileries were no mean home for the governess who wrote Life in the Tuileries under the Second Empire.

Liking the English reticence that prevented Anna fawning over the Prince with the others, Miss Shaw instructed her charge to present her with a flower:

> Of course there was a rush to have it but he held it high above his head ... and ... very gracefully handed it to me. I have kept the faded leaves of that rose, withered like the budding hopes which then surrounded that little royal head.

Miss Shaw did not have an easy time with the rather erratic maternal qualities of the Empress. When the baby Prince was having his first riding lesson, Eugénie whacked the pony with her whip, making him bolt. The riding master succeeded in stopping the pony and brought back the child unhurt.

> ... but he was too angry to remember official decorum, and expressed his feelings with an amount of vigour very unusual in courts, while the English nurse indulged in more respectful lamentations: 'Oh your Majesty! You shouldn't, your Majesty! You've only got *one*, you know.'

The Prince Imperial aged five was in the charge of an English nurse, Miss Shaw, as well as the English governess Anna Bicknell.

Typically Anna's reaction was neither furious nor obsequious, but clear-eyed about the situation: 'It is evident that the Empress in no way intended to risk the life of her child, but she was herself fearless to excess and often thoughtless in the presence of danger. She was determined her son should not be a milk-sop and she did not stop to examine the "fitness of things".'

Anna Bicknell's memoirs present a fascinating picture of Court life of the period, and a touching one of the predicament of the poor Empress Eugénie. Her unconventionality and high spirits obviously chafed at the restrictions and formality:

> The Emperor was benevolent but silent; the Empress tried to talk incessantly with real or feigned vivacity; sometimes, in the young days of the Empire, she proposed dancing and one of the gentlemen present turned the handle of a mechanical piano playing dancing tunes.

The courtiers found these social events a great strain:

> The ladies present remained standing until they were requested to sit down ... The gentlemen, however, stood upright during the whole evening, and many found this a trial. The evenings were very heavy in general, a fact which those admitted to them did not attempt to conceal.

The Empress's worries about her husband's infidelities (Anna commented wryly, 'Usually after taking tea the Emperor retired to "transact business with his private secretary" as was stated; what that "business" was ... had better not be too closely examined'), and the repression demanded by formality seem at times to have given her an almost manic gaiety. The old Duc de Tascher, who suffered from rheumatic gout, would emerge wearily from the Imperial quarters groaning, 'There is no way of inducing the Empress to go to bed!'

With her cheerfulness and tact, Anna became universally popular among the rarefied denizens of the Tuileries: 'the kindness shown to me there ripened into intimacy and confidential friendship'. Private views, the Emperor's box at the theatre, intimate parties with Their Imperial Majesties, she appreciated them all but was never overwhelmed by them, always preserving a calm British detachment. She gives a wonderful vignette of an evening spent with the de Taschers and Madame Ristori, the reigning tragic queen of the stage, which despite some reservations sound an altogether jollier evening than the 'heavy' Imperial soirées. Ristori was late, but 'with a theatrical sense of timing just as some annoyance was felt and expressed, she appeared'.

She was not, said Anna (now an expert in these matters) 'to be mistaken for a gentlewoman, however well she might play queens'. Her full mellow contralto was pleasing to the ear, 'though she threw into everything she said a degree of fire and excitement not usual in general society'. Sometimes the governessy disapproval of the actressy behaviour makes one feel that the formality of Tuileries had influenced Anna a little too much:

> I was particularly amused by one way the tragic queen disposed of the asparagus on her plate. The tips were first daintily cut off; but then a knife held as firmly as her stage dagger gathered them up, while her thumb secured them on the point and thus conveyed them to her lips with great and rapid dexterity.

After dinner the great actress was induced to recite, and it is a wonderful contrast to other reverent contemporary accounts of Ristori's acting to read Miss Bicknell's appraisal: 'I must acknowledge that my first impression on seeing the visitor . . . suddenly rush forward with clasped hands and tragic exclamations was that of a fit of insanity.'

Anna Bicknell must have contributed much to the restricted life of the Tuileries by her humour and capacity to involve herself in whatever occurred. Emmeline Lott, who travelled to Egypt in the early 1860s to be governess to the Infant Pasha, son of the Viceroy of Egypt, was a far uneasier transplant.

She mistrusted foreign food and foreigners, and endured terrible culture shock as she observed the daily life of the odalisques in the harem in Egypt. Only her indomitable sense of her own Englishness enabled her to survive. In her two-volume memoir *The English Governess in Egypt* she describes the warnings of a fellow traveller, Mr Xenos, on her journey out, which would have caused a lesser woman to turn tail for home. It must have been very discouraging to hear: 'I deeply regret that any English lady should have accepted the appointment you have.'

With the benefit of hindsight, Miss Lott is able to tell us that the Ancient Mariner predictions of Mr Xenos all proved accurate. He warned her of 'petty intrigues and court cabals . . . jealousy and corruption' and the possibility of 'strange deaths', citing the examples of 'numerous viceroys who have been falsely reported to have died suddenly of apoplexy; . . . The unfastening of the bolts of the viceregal railway trains; the poisoning of the dates that infant nephews have handed to their viceregal uncles . . .' The food, continued the pessimistic Mr Xenos, 'will be most unpalatable to your taste, even if it does not (of which I entertain great fears) prove most injurious to your health.' According to him absolutely nothing augured well for her.

Emmeline Lott dressed the part in order to enter the harem.

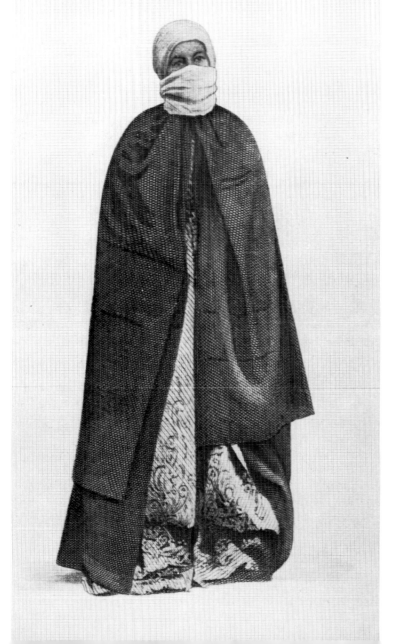

... the entire atmosphere of the Harem is ... impregnated with fumes of tobacco into which powerful narcotics are introduced; ... the loose and uncleanly habits of the attendants ... will disgust you; and the sad monotony of the daily life ... will be of a melancholy convent-like nature ...

But Emmeline kept to her plans, only to find she was billeted with a friend of the Viceroy's until her rooms were ready at the harem. There she was to wait for weeks, until 'I really must have died of ennui'. She loathed the food–'... potatoes, most wretchedly cooked and mutton chops burnt up to a cinder and as hard as leather without a spoonful of gravy or sauce of any kind.'

A Mr HH called to acquaint her with her forthcoming duties. She must have heard an echo of Mr Xenos yet again when he told her that her five-year-old charge 'must never be left alone nor be allowed to partake of any food which has not been previously tasted by ... the Viceregal Doctor'. He also suggested that she accept double wages in exchange for an extra year on her contract, making it three. Emmeline refused and reiterated–with some prescience, as it turned out–that there should be a clause allowing her to retire early in case of ill-health. At last she proceeded by road along the banks of the Nile and then was taken by Viceregal barge and landed on the stairs of the plain E-shaped building which was the harem: 'I ... passed through a small door–the grating sounds of whose rusty hinges still seem to creak in my ears.'

Inside she saw Arabs unloading bales of costly materials, fashionable shoes, wine, tobacco, 'cases of amber mouth-pieces' all 'destined for use of the inmates of that vast conservatory of beauty'. She saw eunuchs, the giant Head Eunuch, the Lady Superintendent of the Slaves (who dripped jewels) and was finally ushered into the presence of the Princess Epouse, mother of the Grand Pasha, to meet her pupil:

At the extremity of those rooms I was led into a smaller apartment, where, on the divan (so called from the Persian word *dive*, signifying 'fairy, gem') which was covered with dirty, faded yellow satin, sat HH the Princess Epouse. She is a wee dwarf of a handsome blonde, with fine blue eyes, short nose, rather large mouth with a fine set of teeth, expressive countenance, but rather sharp and disagreeable voice; her hair was cut in the Savoyard fashion, with two long plaits behind, which were turned round, over the small brown gauze handkerchief she wore round her head, in which were placed, like a band, seven large diamond flies.

She was attired in a dirty, crumpled, light-coloured muslin dress and trousers, sat *à la Turque*, doubled up like a clasped knife, without shoes or stockings, smoking a cigarette. Her waist was encircled with a white gauze handkerchief, having the four corners embroidered with gold thread. It was fastened round, so as to leave two ends hanging down like the lappet of a riding-habit. Her feet were encased in babouches, 'slippers without heels'.

By her side sat HH the Grand Pasha Ibrahim, her son, so styled after the manner adopted by the renowned Mahomet Ali with the Princess Nuzley, '*Nuzley Hanem*'. He was dressed in the uniform of an officer of the Egyptian infantry. On his head he wore the fez; across his shoulder hung a silver-gilt chain, from which was suspended a small silver square box, beautifully chased with cabalistic figures of men, beasts, and trees, enclosed inside which was another smaller box made of cypress-wood which contained verses of the Koran. He was about five years old, of dark complexion, short Arab nose, and rather tall for his age, and looked the very picture of a happy, round-faced cherub. When I approached towards the Divan, he gave full proof that his lungs were in a healthy state, as he set up a most hideous shriek, buried his black head in his mother's lap, who laughed most heartily at the strange reception His Highness had thought proper to bestow upon his future governess.

The English Governess in Egypt, *Miss Lott's two-volume memoir, makes much of her inside knowledge of the harem, as did many other travellers of the time, but this picture shows that visits to harems by European ladies were, if not commonplace, hardly unique. It appeared in an* Illustrated London News *of the period.*

From then on it was a more or less unremitting process of disillusionment, except Miss Lott complains with such gusto that one feels there is pleasure in the process. The first disappointment was the ladies of the harem, in whom she 'failed to find the slightest trace of loveliness'. Nor did her attitude mellow after longer exposure to them; her later description of a typical day in the harem is redolent with disapproval. Apparently these Princesses spent most of the time 'doubling themselves up on divans' wearing 'dirty filthy muslin dresses'. At dawn they started smoking strong Turkish cigarettes and drinking strong Turkish coffee, 'then they remained quite motionless, apparently in a dreamy state as they never uttered a syllable'. Slaves brought them small silver pans of water, pieces of rag and balls of soap for their morning toilette, and then to Miss Lott's evident relief they cleaned their teeth 'with toothbrushes and powder of French manufacture'. Hair-care was another matter:

They only combed their hair once a week . . . and, pardon me, but 'murder will out', the members of the vermin family which were removed from it were legion!

After a twenty-minute breakfast of all the foods Emmeline had come to detest, they settled down to smoke opium:

Often times after the Princesses had been indulging too freely in that habit, to which they had become slaves, their countenances would assume most hideous aspects, their eyes glared, their eyebrows were knit closely together, no one dared to approach them. In fact they had all the appearance of mad creatures . . .

GOVERNESSES

A siesta followed, from which they rose at 5 p.m. to perform their evening toilette,

> which consisted in merely changing their outer garments and attiring themselves in *new* muslin dresses as they never wear them after they have been washed . . . hence the consumption of clothing of every description was enormous.

Supper was the same unvarying menu of 'greasy foods', 'which they eat like beasts of the field'. The Princesses spent their evenings playing dominoes; listening to 'lascivious tales' about 'women and their immoralities'; eating sweetmeats, drinking yet more coffee and smoking yet more cigarettes. At ten o'clock they went to bed. It was not Miss Lott's idea of a day well spent, and she obviously preferred the occasions when His Highness the Viceroy informed them of his intention to visit:

> It seemed like a pantomimic feat; as if harlequin with his magic wand had touched them all with his galvanic battery, for in the twinkling of an eye their dirty soiled and crumpled muslins, their Monmouth Street and Petticoat Lane finery was exchanged for gorgeous silks and glittering diamonds.

The slaves were another worry. They had greeted her with enthusiasm, kissing her hands and feet, they had been fascinated by her straw hat and crinoline, and Miss Lott had even managed to give them lessons in deportment 'in order that they might see how European ladies generally paced up and down their rooms'. But although she managed to overlook whatever HH Viceroy did with the Princesses, she was not convinced that the eunuchs were sexually irreproachable: 'having myself witnessed several of these spectres of mankind "toying and wooing" with the black female slaves, I doubted their infirmity of body and kept a watchful eye over them.'

Her food and her accommodation are a running lamentation through her narrative, from her first sight of her apartment:

> . . . a total absence of all the appendages necessary for a lady's bedroom–not even a vase . . . yet what could I have expected, as every apartment which I had passed through was totally destitute of everything that ought to have been placed therein?

It seems a little insular to complain of the absence of footstools, pianos and music stools (as she proceeds to do) but it was clearly unbearable for a status-conscious governess to be expected 'to clean my own room and wash my own linen, both of which I resolutely refused to do'. Worst of all, she found was was to eat her meals with Clara the German maid:

> This was treatment I had never expected to receive . . . Fati-

122

gue, disgust and vexation at the accommodation which had
been provided for me had almost taken away all my appetite;
but at the sight of the Arab dishes I turned quite sick . . .
I hastily retired to my miserable pallet . . .

The young Grand Pasha was not an easy proposition, either.
She was determined to run a recognizable 'Viceregal nursery'
but there were many battles to be fought first. The table-
manners were horrifying to Miss Lott:

> Here and there lay morsels which had been torn asunder from
> the joint or bird and being unsuited to the palate . . . had
> been thrown down . . . in short, it presented a sight that would
> make the stomach of a cook-shop carver heave again.

Bed-time was a distressingly un-English ritual. The Pasha was
dressed in his nightclothes and then a silver brazier filled with
charcoal was brought into the room:

> In it was thrown a quantity of wood of aloes, aromatic gum
> and lumps of crystallised sugar. Then the head-nurse lifted
> up His Highness in her powerful arms and swung him round
> it nine times while she counted that number aloud in Turkish.

Meanwhile, HH Princess Epouse sat on the divan, smoking
cigarettes.

Miss Lott took it upon herself to try to discipline her charge
according to English traditions but it was uphill work. Indulging in a temper tantrum when three gardeners made him a
bouquet that was not to his taste, he destroyed the flowers and
ordered the gardeners thrashed by his eunuchs.

> This they continued doing for some time; but as the Prince
> made no sign to them to discontinue the chastisement I began
> to remonstrate with him at such a display of his ungovernable
> temper . . . This incident clearly gave me an insight into the
> Prince's character which was evidently as cruel, overbearing
> and brutal as that of his grandfather, Ibrahim Pasha, whose
> private life was disgraced by the most barbarous pastimes.

There was plenty of other evidence of such disconcerting behaviour, such as when a slave girl stole some sweetmeats:

> H.H. the Princess Epouse, upon being informed of it, ordered
> the girl to be punished; but H.H. the Grand Pasha put himself
> into such a paroxysm of rage that he lay upon the floor and
> foamed at the mouth exclaiming at intervals that she should
> *not* be punished except by *himself*; and nothing would satisfy
> him until his mother had countermanded the order.

The irregularity of the domestic arrangements at the harem

were a permanent source of frustration to Miss Lott, who could not organize a satisfactory educational system for her charge:

> Sometimes I received orders . . . at the caprice of H.H. the Princess Epouse who, as a matter of course, was perfectly ignorant as to the manner adopted in Europe of training up young children, to take the Grand Pasha out walking at six in the morning; on other occasions at seven, eight and nine o'clock. And when once the little Prince was in the gardens it was exceedingly difficult to get him to return . . . no matter how singular and unreasonable his whims were, still he must be indulged in them.

She drew up a scheme for his education but the Viceroy would not sanction it, explaining he did not wish the Prince to be taught from books or toys, as he would pick up English quickly enough by being constantly with Miss Lott. She conceded sadly, 'I abandoned all idea of educational training.'

Eventually she was worn by ill-health and depression almost amounting to a nervous breakdown. She gave in her resignation which was accepted. Who knows if they were sorry to see her go? She claims she never offended anyone despite her innate disapproval of almost everything, but one wonders if her condescending version of events might not be just a little self-deceiving:

> The whole of the inmates of the Harem soon began thoroughly to appreciate my European ways and habits . . . and did their best, poor ignorant and deluded creatures, to abandon any habits which I explained to them were repugnant to delicacy . . .

Governesses tried hard to avoid such humiliations as those which befell the Australian immigrants in this engraving, who were effectively auctioned off to prospective employers.

The anonymous authoress of *Recollections of a Royal Governess*, Miss M—, had as shaky a start to her adventures as Emmeline Lott. She seems too xenophobic a character to leave home successfully. She had language difficulties en route for Poland, displayed considerable impatience with foreigners ('suspicion [was] written on every line of his foreign countenance') and managed to lose her luggage. But the family at her first–non-royal–post at Castle Büsk were kind and welcoming. In fact, the manners of Count and Countess Badeni and their daughter Wanda convinced Miss M that the bluer the blood the kinder the reception of the governess: 'they have all treated me as an honoured guest . . . It just shows that the higher one goes, the more considerate the treatment.'

She was impressed by the grandeur of the castle and by the glass-houses for violets alone, the lawns, the beautifully kept flower beds, the pineapple house, the vineries, tennis courts, poultry houses and dovecotes. Breakfast was a most unEnglish meal: 'a . . . Gargantuan feast! There was cold game, meat, eggs, foie gras and caviare!'

Her duties were light and she revelled in the feudal life of the castle. She was wakened by the roaring of stags fighting in the park–'the noise of the blows of one head against another was appalling . . . but the trees were so thick that it was only a few shadowy and phantom-like glimpses I could catch.' There were boar hunts, where the party wore white cloth costumes and white felt boots to camouflage them in the snow. Miss M had a thoroughly English reaction to the shooting of foxes–she was deeply shocked by what she considered an unsporting act, thereby losing her chances of a fur coat: 'Wanda told me later that I lost those skins by my surprise.'

One of the pleasures of these memoirs is the blossoming of Miss M's curiosity and bravery. The Countess was a swashbuckling figure and swept Miss M along in her wake. Once there was a thrilling excursion across the frontier to Russia with the Countess and her friends, who exhibited a noble disdain for the formality of passports. Miss M quaked while the Cossack border guards debated and then (presumably charmed by the Countess and the grandeur of her party) let them through. They continued under the surveillance of twelve mounted Cossacks who 'dashed about like wild creatures . . . treating us to a display of horsemanship more marvellous than I have ever dreamed of.' When Miss M realized that the Countess was smuggling out Russian tobacco for a wager she was shocked, but it is an indication of her new perspective when she sums it up as '. . . an exciting and nerve wracking experience, but I would not have missed it on any account.'

Soon she was formulating her own escapist expeditions. She made an illicit visit to the Volks Theatre in 'a low part of Lemberg', where she felt conspicuous and panicky, for not just the audience but all the actors stared at her. She enjoyed the play, *A Peasants Tragedy*, understanding through gesture and facial expression rather than words, and was surprised by the Polish response. There was 'no applause, but long and distinctly audible sighs and the occasional laugh were the only encouragement the actors received'. As she left, the police swooped on the departing crowd, hustling away a youth and a girl 'because there was more anarchism rife than usual'. Miss M felt the hostility of the crowd, who thought she was a spy, and realizing she must get away or be mobbed she fled back to the castle. A few days later she was gently reprimanded by the Count, who knew all about her escapade and warned her against any more, explaining that 'it was only through the intervention of two secret service men in my employ that you are not now lying in the citadel'.

After two happy years in Poland, her next post was understandably anticlimactic. She became governess to the daughters of Countess Antonelli of Ceccano, a small medieval town between Rome and Naples. Miss M is brisk about the failure of this enterprise: it is a great contrast to the elaborate lamentations of Emmeline Lott: 'There are some people whom it is impossible to get on with, no matter how hard one may try. The Countess Antonelli was one of these.'

Fortunately, friends arranged her appointment as English governess to the Archduchess Elizabeth Marie, the only child of the late Archduke Rudolf and grand-daughter of the Emperor of Austria. It was the summit of Miss M's ambition, 'as I always told you I meant to be in a Royal family,' and a happy release from the demanding Countess Antonelli: 'The joy of my appointment was only equalled by my pleasure at leaving Ceccano.'

The sixteen-year-old Archduchess had very much disliked Miss M's English predecessor at the Château Impérial, Laxenburg, Austria, so the first challenge was to win the confidence of her charge. It seems to have been something of an endurance test to establish the relationship on a good footing. 'By now the Archduchess had recovered from her first shyness and criticised my hat with great frankness.'

Miss M may even have reconsidered some of her preconceptions about the perfection of royalty when she was out in a rowing boat with her new pupil:

> The Archduchess was in great spirits and splashed water over us all. I concluded that one of my duties was to sit still and look pleasant while I was being drenched. The kind of humour which consists in making people thoroughly wet and uncomfortable for one's amusement seems to be a brand peculiar to Eastern Europe–that is as regards the upper sections of society!

But it was not long before Miss M brought her influence to bear. She taught an opportune lesson to the Archduchess when they found a stray young wild cat nearly dead with hunger and carried it back with them to the castle. Tea was waiting on silver trays, a separate silver service for each of them. The Archduchess gave the cat her cream, saying she herself would use half of Miss M's.

This was an excellent opportunity for a moral lesson, so I told her that if she gave the cream she must herself do without it. That she must do without anything was an idea so new to her that it was fairly staggering. However, she agreed and we gravely drank our tea, *sans* milk.

The English governess who had preceded Miss M had clearly made very little educational headway with the Archduchess, for she could write and spell no better than a child of six. 'Poor little neglected thing,' wrote Miss M when she received the following postcard from Munich:

I am vel, it es beutiful, mach perfier dan en Wienna. Wienna es in compareson hored - Elizabeth.

It cannot be said that Miss M triumphed over Elizabeth's literacy problems, although she professed to find this later letter a great improvement:

Like Maria Graham, Miss M had to deal with the formality of Court life and its intrigues. Although they all lived under one roof in the castle, 'we received and paid our visits to one another exactly as if we were three miles apart.' Her charge taught her the appropriate curtsies for different ranks–'"This for Grandpa–this for Mamma, and this for me!" And it is very quaint to see her watch me when I meet her mother. Of course none of the other ladies knows she does this, and she loves the secret.'

The Austrian Court was a minefield of scandal and gossip. Miss M enjoyed the stories of Elizabeth's aunt, the vain, shallow Princess Louise, who conducted an overt affair with her riding master and exercised courtiers' tongues with her extravagance. 'We heard stories of her buying 16 hats and 15 pairs of costly corsets at one time.'

The death of Elizabeth's father had been a scandalous one, popularly believed to be a lovers' suicide pact, and every year the Imperial Household attended an anniversary Mass. The Archduchess Elizabeth would never participate properly, and all Miss M could ever elicit from her was the statement, 'But it was not Papa I saw lying-in-state. Papa is not dead.'

The Grand Duchess Olga, in the charge of the English Miss Eagar, drew this picture of her mother the Czarina which somehow her governess brought back home with her on her return in 1904.

Elizabeth's grandmother, the Empress Elizabeth, kept herself entirely remote from her grand-daughter, her mother neglected her, only her grandfather the Emperor showed her affection. No wonder Miss M became the focus of the young girl's emotions. It must have been a terrible wrench for both of them when the Archduchess was considered of an age to dispense with a governess and to have her own suite of ladies-in-waiting. She gave the departing Miss M many presents, including a gold bracelet set with sapphires and diamonds ('The handsomest piece of jewellery I have ever had') but one feels that Miss M probably preferred the double framed pictures of Elizabeth in her first communion dress and in ordinary dress. '"This", she said, pointing to the demure figure kneeling on the *prie-dieu*, "is me when I'm good. This," pointing to the other which looked out of the frame with wide dancing eyes, "is me when I'm naughty."'

There were four young children in the Czar's household at St Petersburg, 'one of the most insanitary towns in Europe' in Miss Eagar's opinion. Fortunately she was able to summer in Peterhof where the governess had her own villa.

Miss M Eagar, who in 1899 travelled to St Petersburg to be Imperial Governess to the daughters of the last and tragic Tsar, Nicholas II, was as susceptible to the idea of royalty as Miss M, but her book *Six Years at the Russian Court* is a much duller memoir, for she never lapses into indiscretion. Her impressions of the family are an unadulterated paean of praise. The Empress, who was 'the handsomest woman I had ever seen', received her in her boudoir, 'a lovely room', and herself introduced Miss Eagar to her charges, 'beautifully dressed . . . in transparent white muslin dresses trimmed with Brussels lace and worn over pale-blue satin slips'. The three-year-old Grand Duchess was 'a very fine child', eighteen-month Grand Duchess Tatiana 'a very pretty child, remarkably like her mother, but delicate in appearance'.

The Winter Palace was full of astonishing treasures including 'the finest set of Rembrandts extant', but doubts are raised about Miss Eagar's capacity for culture when we read that she looked at a Rembrandt 'trying to make out what it means', and her only observation about the picture gallery was:

They are all arranged according to schools, Dutch school etc all together. So one gets sacred subjects mixed up with many very different pictures.

Easter was spent at Tsarskoe Selo in the Little Palace, built for Alexander I. Miss Eagar approved of the nurseries–'very fine, consisting of about eleven rooms. In the bathroom is a stationary bath of solid silver, used for the bigger children. There is a small bath for the use of whatever baby reigns. Each child's name is engraved upon it, so it forms a historical record.'

But she did not approve of the 'thousands of coloured eggs which are indispensable to a Russian Easter' since they caused chaos in her orderly kingdom:

We used to colour a couple of hundred every Good Friday in the nurseries. It was a great pleasure to the children but rather dirty work.

Each May they used to go to Peterhof, where Miss Eagar had her own villa, a little rococo house built and furnished in First Empire style. It sounds as if the little Grand Duchesses had a happy and free childhood:

One of the delights of the children was to go there to spend the afternoon and take tea, especially during hay-making time, when they would have rides in the haycocks and run up and down the grassy slopes. Another great delight was to visit the farm, see the cows milked, feed the fowls, collect eggs and fill baskets with apples . . . The farmer's wife . . . was bringing up by hand four kittens whose mother had been killed. When the little Grand Duchesses went over in the morning on their Shetland ponies or bicycles, the kittens were always brought out, four bottles of milk were produced and each child, bottle of milk in one hand and a kitten comfortably tucked under her arm, would quietly take a place in the milk-cart and go for a drive round the farm-yards, feeding the kittens in the meantime.

It is somehow comforting to know that the children who met such a mysterious and tragic end had halcyon summer days together under the watchful eye of Miss Eagar. They were a loving, united family, and there is a very touching description of the Grand Duchess Olga insisting on making the typically English nursery Christmas present for her father–a kettle-holder. 'It had a little kettle singing on a fire and "Polly put the kettle on" worked on it.' Miss Eagar added a ruche of blue ribbon, feeling that perhaps it was not the most suitable gift for the Tsar of All The Russias.

There is more in the memoirs about Court festivities than nursery life. Despite her judgement that 'St Petersburg is . . . the most unsanitary town in Europe. The drainage is defective and the habits are not healthy,' Miss Eagar was always on hand to record the lavishness of the occasions with admiration. The opening ball of the St Petersburg season was gargantuan in scale; the supper rooms were arranged like gardens and the tables groaned with food. Miss Eagar records that 350 dishes of chicken, 350 large lobsters with mayonnaise sauce, 350 tongues, 350 plates of assorted meats, hundreds of gallons of soup and 2,000 bunches of asparagus were disposed of, not to mention fruit, wine, cakes, biscuits, ices, creams and jellies. She observed thoughtfully, 'A ball at the Palace is good for trade in St Petersburg.'

Miss Eagar's horizons were bounded by the palace. She ruled the nursery hierarchy, vetting the suitors of the nursery maids; nursed the Grand Duchess Olga through typhoid; marvelled at the splendour and extravagance of the Empress's wardrobe–it would have been too much to expect her to have any intimations of revolution.

The status of the governess required that she had to ring the servants' bell.

> Russia has a kind of local government but until the people are better educated it seems to me that a constitution cannot benefit them much. They are not capable of guiding them-selves. The little nursery party in Tsarskoe Selo would be just as well able to arrange their daily life without the aid of 'grown-ups' as are the Russians in general.

But in 1904 the Tsarevitch was born–the long-awaited son. Miss Eagar had never been in sole control of her charges' education (there were special tutors for subjects beyond her range) and the arrival of the future ruler of Russia precipitated a reorganization of the nursery. The last Imperial Governess at the Court of St Petersburg returned to England with her memories. How she must have grieved at the news of the assas-sination of 'her' dear family at Ekaterinburg in 1918.

These women disseminated the arcane traditions of the English nursery schoolroom all over the world. It is strange to think just where the kettle-holders and flower-pressing books might be found, just who learnt the nursery rhymes and received the deportment lessons. The 'English Miss' was an Empire-builder in her way.

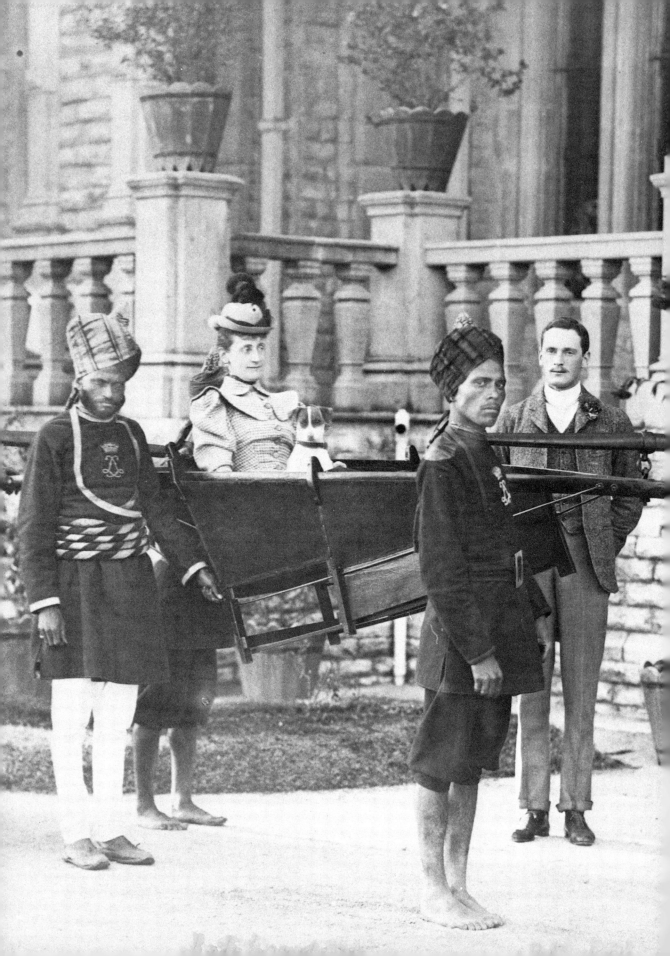

CHAPTER 6

MEMSAHIBS

Lady Lansdowne enjoyed a spin in a palanquin, particularly when in the hands of these two handsome fellows. She had this photograph taken at Simla in 1890. She was the wife of the Fifth Marquess of Lansdowne, Viceroy of India 1886–1893.

The life of the Englishwoman in India was inextricably linked with the Englishman who ruled there. For more than two centuries India was subjected to an avalanche of wives, daughters, sisters and prospective brides from England; appendages to the Empire Builders. Even when independent solo women travellers seemed to be circling the globe elsewhere, in India they were a rarity, and spinster teachers and missionaries were considered a separate caste by family-orientated expatriate Anglo-Indians.

From the middle of the eighteenth century, the East India Company imported women as chattels for the marriage-market, as the Portuguese at Goa had done before them. They guaranteed the girls' board and lodging for one year, threatening them with an ignominious return home if they were not married by then. Though it sounds vaguely barbaric, it was still in vogue more than a hundred years later, as sheltered young middle-class girls flocked to India in the hope of finding imperialist husbands. They were unkindly labelled 'the Fishing Fleet' and James Morris encapsulated their lives in *Farewell the Trumpets*:

> [they] all too often returned sad-eyed and sallow, when 30 years later their husbands reluctantly retired at last and they settled alien and out of touch at Guildford or Yelverton, all their imperial pretensions crumbled, all their memories rather a bore. No wonder in their exiled prime they were often supercilious and overbearing: there was purpose to their husbands' imperialism, fun too, very often, but there was not much satisfaction to their own.

The memsahib became an easy target for mockery. There is plenty of evidence to build up a portrait of a snobbish, racially-prejudiced Englishwoman abroad who imposed her tastes, disregarded the natives, disdained the language, mismanaged her household and spoiled her children. Homesickness permeated the monotony of station life and she wrote intermi-

nable letters home, complaining of the customs, the heat and
the smells. She whiled away the enervating hours with tatting
and embroidery and recorded her impressions in endless water-
colours (which although intended simply to pass the time have
left us with a fascinating record of the minutae of the Raj ladies'
lives, like the previously unpublished sketches of Mrs Mary Car-
lisle made in the 1860s which are printed here). The undemand-
ing domesticity sharpened the memsahibs' need for distraction
out of the home. The missionary Henrietta Streatfield tells the
cautionary tale of 'Norah' in her book *Glimpses of Indian Life*
(1908):

> To tell the truth, at that moment the young wife was
> decidedly homesick, and a great longing for her dear ones,
> so far away, swept over her. When her husband was with
> her she seemed to want nothing else; but he was busy and
> out a great deal; and now he would be for ten days away

*A lady authoress writing in 1839 to
those about to become memsahibs
advised ladies 'to study drawing under
a good master and understand the
principles of the art; for there is little
in the way of tuition to be had in
India'. These six drawings are from
the pencil of Mrs M Carlyle, the wife
of Captain Anthony Carlyle of the
60th. They left India in 1872.*

in camp, and this might often happen. 'If I had one of the girls with me while he was away, I shouldn't mind,' she thought; 'but to be quite alone! what shall I do? There seems nothing to be done here. Even one of the home dogs would be a companion. How stupid I am! I must not give way and be foolish; I must make some interests, and after all, what a lucky girl I am to have such a husband!' and brushing away a tear, she rose, and calling "Boy," proceeded with that worthy to the store-room, there to give out the stores for the day (a daily duty in India). This includes grain for the horses, oil for the lamps; in fact, everything that can be needed in the house and stables. That done, and her orders given for the day, she interviewed her malis (gardeners) about preparing some beds she wished to have sown with seeds from home. She then decided to begin her letter to the home circle, though it wanted four days to mail day–but she would write a journal letter, and tell them all all about her new life. She wondered what there would be to tell during the next ten days! Letters and 'chits' to the club, stores and bazaar, took up the rest of the morning, and at 12.30 it was tiffin time. After that she would lie down for an hour, and take a book–it seemed the right thing to do in India, though as she was well and strong she hardly seemed to need the rest. However, Arthur wished it, and that was enough. Over her book she fell asleep, to wake up and find it half-past three, and nearly tea time. Getting up she dressed, and was ready when at four o'clock her husband came in. Tea over, they drove off to the golf links. 'You must try and get a round every day for exercise,' he said, as they spun along in the high dog cart. 'This is important out here to keep in good health.'

'Golf is lovely when I have you to go round the links with,' she answered; 'but when you are away I think a drive is all I shall care for. It is no fun going round alone.'

'Oh! you will soon make friends,' he said, 'and have plenty of people to play with. Mrs Innis and Mrs Gordon are capital players, and would welcome you, I am sure.'

The game over, they drove to the club and dismissed the carriage. 'Will you be ready by eight o'clock?' she asked, as he left her to go off to the billiard room.

'About that time, I should think,' was his answer, and she sauntered into the ladies' room. One or two nodded to her as she came in, but nearly all were playing bridge, and were quite engrossed in their game. She sat down and looked at the papers, and from time to time exchanged a few words with the two ladies who were not playing.

A young Mrs Jardine, also a bride, she rather liked; she was so amusing and full of life. She was listening to the story of a carriage accident the week before, given in that young lady's most graphic style, when the latter was called off to the Bridge table, and Norah was left alone, trying to be interested in the *Queen* and other papers, which she had seen before. So far she had resisted the fascination of Bridge.

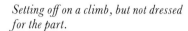

Norah's fate (deeply disapproved of by the author) was to succumb to the iniquitous fascination of playing bridge for money:

> At the end of the week she gave in; she decided that even
> her mother would prefer her playing Bridge for points, rather
> than having nothing to do, and never joining the other ladies
> in the station it seemed the only thing, if she wished to be
> sociable. In writing home she did not mention the subject,
> fearing to pain her mother, and feeling that she would never
> understand the life of a station in India, unless she had lived
> in it, and so knew its utter lack of interest and variety.
>
> Today Norah —— is one of the best and keenest lady
> Bridge players in her station.

Others filled the daily void with snobbish gossip. At this period
the nick-name of the ladies' drawing-room at the United Service
Club in Simla was 'the snakepit'. But it was a much older tradition and not confined exclusively to women, as William Hickey's
Calcutta memoirs (1749–90) amply demonstrate:

> Lady Anstruther paid Lady Russell the utmost attention
> upon her first arrival, but within a twelvemonth she became
> so extremely jealous of the universal respect and esteem Lady
> Russell was held in by both male and female, that to speak
> well of her in her [Lady Anstruther's] presence was sure to

'Fears are entertained for the safety of the "cellar".'

excite her enmity. Those therefore, who like me, were intimate in Sir Henry Russell's family were always liable to be coldly received if not insulted at Lady Anstruther's. It fell to my lot to be longer in experiencing the capricious woman's impertinence than many of my acquaintances; it however came at last, for upon my going to one of her public nights accompanied by young Henry Russell, she was so pointedly rude to us both that I resolved never again to enter her door, nor did I, although I continued to receive cards of invitation to dinner and to evening parties, for many months subsequent to my absenting myself. As I have already said, she was the most capricious, and to those who would submit to it, at times the most over-bearing insolent woman, notwithstanding which, from her elevated station and the splendour of her entertainments, everybody almost submitted to her impertinence, continuing to court her. The leading men of the Settlement now and then complained that Sir John Anstruther's wines were not so good as they ought to be. Some of the wags of Calcutta who had remarked that Sir Henry Russell's claret was always of the very best, while his dinners were execrable, therefore proposed that Sir John Anstruther should be recommended to employ Sir Henry Russell's wine merchant, and that Sir Henry Russell should be equally urged to engage Sir John Anstruther's cook. Doctor Fleming of gormandizing celebrity made the following facetious distich extempore upon the fare of the two houses.

'To dine with the Judges is no great recreation;
The one gives you poison! The other starvation.'

But it must not be forgotten that these complaining, bridge-playing, gossiping memsahibs gave up their youth, their health and most of the pleasures of motherhood, since their children were educated in England. Many lost babies: the combination of incompetence and hostile conditions created an exceedingly high infant mortality rate. They faced squalor, discomfort and the possibility of death daily–and all for an imperialist ideal in which they played no active part.

But among this sad sisterhood there are plenty of glittering exceptions; indeed it is their caustic pens which often drew the picture of the discredited, stereotyped memsahib! Among the first wave of English transplants to India was Mrs Eliza Fay (1756–1815). In eighteenth-century Calcutta the English were no longer just traders and soldiers but acquiring racial consciousness and a sense of imperial responsibility. It was not the hidebound zealotry of the later Victorian rule–the Georgians were more robust–but it established social consequences and the tentative birth of Viceregal airs and graces. A social routine evolved which partially survived until the departure of the British from India. Mrs Fay was very well equipped to comment on it. Neither high-born nor an intellectual, she is an eager observer and utterly without pretension. As EM Forster says in his introduction to her *Letters from India* (published in 1925 by Leonard and Virginia Woolf):

> Were she only frank and naive, it would be something, but she is much more, a soul courageous and gallant, an eye, an ear always on the watch. She does not conceal her sufferings, but not once does she whine over them . . .

Mrs Fay's origins are obscure but her letters were written when she was twenty-three and recently married to Anthony Fay, a lawyer who was going out to practise as an advocate at the Supreme Court of Calcutta. The journey out–crammed with incident–immediately makes it clear that Eliza was of sterner stuff than the wilting stereotype. From Cairo she wrote: 'I have found scarce any inconvenience from the heat, though all of our party who have been in India agree that they never felt the weather so oppressively hot as here.' She succumbed to fever, swiftly recovered, and travelled across the desert to Suez (this was before the Canal), behaving, Mr Fay said, 'most courageously'. Displaying not a vestige of mock modesty, Eliza goes further:

> I bore the fatigues of the desert like a lion . . . We have been pillaged of almost everything by the Arabs. This is the paradise of thieves, I think the whole population may be divided into two classes of them; those who adopt force and those who effect their purpose by fraud.

Eliza Fay's letters are a somewhat acidic account of life in India, for there was nothing genteel about her.

In fact, there is nothing genteel about her. She suffers when she is treated snobbishly by fellow travellers in Cairo but adopts no false refinement: she is a born survivor. On board ship to Calcutta on the last phase of the journey, provisions ran short and she writes, '. . . we are grown quite savages; two or three of us perhaps fighting for a bone; for there is no respect of persons.'

They had an unnerving first encounter with Calcutta: arriving in a canoe through the surf ('so that we reached the shore dripping wet'), they were imprisoned by Hyder Ali for 'fifteen weeks . . . in wretched confinement, totally in the power of Barbarians.' Bribes failed, and finally an advocate called Mr Isaac secured their release, causing Mrs Fay to give vent to a torrent of pro-Semitic thanks. She was free of fashionable racism, and it is no surprise to read her views on Europeans and Hindus when she reaches Madras:

> . . . you behold Europeans languishing under various complaints which they call incidental to the climate, an assertion it would ill become a stranger like myself to controvert, but respecting which I am a little sceptical; because I see very plainly that the same mode of living would produce the same effects even 'in the hardy regions of the North'. You may like-

wise perceive that human nature has its faults and follies eveywhere, and that *black* rogues are as common as white ones . . . I wish these people would not vex one by their tricks; for there is something in the mild countenances and gentle manners of the Hindoos that interests me exceedingly.

Clearly, Mrs Fay was not popular with other more orthodox expatriates. She sketches a vivid and acid portrait of the snobbish Mrs Hastings in Calcutta, who 'expects to be treated with the most profound respect and deference,' and had the temerity to hint that Eliza might have brought about her own misfortunes by 'imprudently venturing on such an expedition out of mere curiosity'. It is a little hard to believe that Eliza only '*slightly* touched on the misfortunes which had befallen me': she had obviously been bragging at length about her adventures, but it is game, set and match to Mrs Fay when she describes her hostess's hairstyle:

Her appearance is rather eccentric, owing to the circumstance of her beautiful auburn hair being disposed in ringlets, throwing an air of elegant, nay almost infantine simplicity over the countenance . . .

'A New Year's Day . . . [with] garlands hanging round our necks.'

She must have been something of a thorn in the flesh at a conventional tea-party. Naturally Englishwomen were horrified by

the Indian tradition of *suttee*, the custom of widows burning themselves with the dead bodies of their husbands. Mrs Fay (perhaps rather embittered on the subject of marriage by this time, since her husband had left her) writes:

> . . . so much are we the slaves of habit *everywhere* that were it necessary for a woman's reputation to burn herself in England, many a one who has accepted a husband merely for the sake of an establishment . . . would yet mount the funeral pile with all imaginable decency and die with heroic fortitude.

It is difficult to lay aside Mrs Fay's letters. They are historically interesting but their main charm is in their revelation of character. EM Forster says, 'Her opinions and desires are always sticking out . . . and ripping the chaste mantle of literature.'

William Hickey was a contemporary of Eliza Fay in Calcutta and his *Memoirs* provide many vignettes of unconventional women, like the outspoken Miss Seymour who was the bastard daughter of Sir George Dallas and a 'native woman of Hindustan who was so fair that this young lady had not the slightest tinge of even the copper-coloured skin'. According to Hickey, she was an exceedingly clever girl 'and a by no means contemptible poetess'. He was rather charmed by her raffishness when she proposed that she should stay unchaperoned in the house he shared with Sir Henry Russell, but more orthodox Raj standards finally prevailed:

William Hickey's Calcutta memoirs written during the latter half of the eighteenth century give vivid pen portraits of the earlier memsahibs.

> 'But, my dear Miss Seymour' (said Mrs Smith, in the presence of Sir Henry Russell), 'do you think it will be quite correct for you, a smart young lady, to take up your abode without any other female in the house with two gentlemen?' 'Dear me,' replied she, 'why not? I am sure I shall not have the least objection, nor can I conceive any reason why I should not, for you know, ma'am, Sir Henry Russell is a grave and learned judge, and Mr. Hickey is an old man!' Sir Henry, who seemed somewhat hurt at being thus spoken of, rather tartly said, 'But give me leave to observe, young Madam, whatever you may think, or affect to think, that both old men and judges are still men, have the failings of men, and there might be more danger than you are aware of.' 'Well, never mind that; that's my business,' said the lively girl, 'I shall not be at all afraid to make the trial, as I do not see any danger, nor will I even lock my chamber door.' As far as I was concerned I was ready and willing to admit the fairness of the lady's argument, and solicited that she might be allowed to follow her inclination, but the correct Mrs Smith, and equally chaste Sir Henry Russell, who really appeared to be more alarmed at such an idea than even Mrs Smith was, pronounced the thing absolutely impossible and must not be thought of.

Another tantalizing character who appears briefly amongst Hickey's bevy of memsahibs is the dashing Mrs Bristow, whose high spirits 'frequently led her into extravagancies and follies of rather too masculine a nature'. She rode astride, winning against experienced jockeys (for she 'would leap over any hedge or ditch that even the most zealous sportsmen were dubious of attempting'); she was a first rate shot, and best of all, she 'understood the present fashionable science of pugilism and would without hesitation knock a man down if he presumed to offer her the slightest insult.' Hickey was plainly quite won over by this hearty girl: '. . . she stopped at nothing that met her fancy, however wild or eccentric, executing whatever she attempted with a *naivete* and ease and elegance that was irresistible'.

'Bungalow of an English coffee planter.'

However, the spirit of Queen Victoria pervaded the next generation of women, who went to India in the 1830s: these memsahibs brought with them the sense of duty and self-righteousness that afflicted the High Victorians. But Emily Eden was of the Regency, with its more full-blooded implications, even though it was 1835 when she accompanied her brother Lord Auckland to India where he had been appointed Governor-General. Both his unmarried sisters, Emily and Fanny, reluctantly gave up their cultivated aristocratic life in England to accompany him. They spent six years in India: Emily's letters home (collected under the title *Up The Country* in 1866) describe the range of their experiences. There was the stiff Anglo-Indian world of dinners and balls, gloomily recorded as 'The dinners certainly are endless,' or 'We had our ball on Thursday–a particularly sleepy one.'

A contemporary letter-writer (recently published) was Mrs Isabella Fane, whose description of the Misses Eden in Calcutta in 1896 is an unexpected one: 'We got on famously. They are both great talkers, both old, both ugly and both s . . . k like polecats!'

But Miss Fane's enthusiasm was not reciprocated. Emily did not find the European women of Calcutta stimulating company: '. . . there is not anybody I can prefer to any other body . . . there is a *morne* feeling at the end of their visit that it will be tiresome when it comes round to their turn of coming again.' She did what she could to loosen the corsets of bureaucracy which bound the Anglo-Indian society: she came from that charmed inner circle of the aristocracy which usually gets what it wants. Setting off 'up the country' for a two and a half year tour, she cut through the red tape of the Raj that accompanied the Governor-General's triumphal progress. Seeing a great fair for horses at Bullhga, she persuaded her brother George to go:

The ladies of Simla passed the time as if they were still in Surrey, indulging in such exciting pastimes as fancy dress. The Black Hearts were very rich bachelors, and one year the prizes for the 'marvellous Black Hearts fancy dress ball' were fetched from Paris!

> . . . but we had hardly landed when A came breathless from the other steamer to say that Mr B and Mr C were both half mad at the idea of a Governor-General going on shore in this way, and that C was actually dancing about the deck with rage; and A wanted us to turn back and give it up. Luckily, G would not be advised to do this. They said we should be murdered amongst other things; but in my life I never saw such a civil, submissive set of people. Our people and the police of the place walked on first, desiring the crowd to sit down, which they all did instantly, crouching together and making a lane all through the fair. They are civil creatures, and I am very fond of the natives. There were a great many

thousands of them, and some beautiful costumes; the bazaars were full of trinkets, and pretty shawls and coloured cottons. We went in our tonjauns, and G walked till he was tired, which is soon done; and A left us quite satisfied as to our safety, and almost persuaded it was a dignified measure. We wanted him to tell C that he had left G in one of the 'merry-go-rounds', of which there were several, but it was not a subject that admitted of levity. B said the Governor-General should never appear publicly without a regiment, and that there was no precedent for his going to Bullhga fair. I told him we had made a precedent, and that it would be his duty to take the next Governor-General, be he ever so lame or infirm, to this identical fair.

The Edens also moved in a world of nawabs and maharajahs, bejewelled princes who pressed lavish presents upon them. Protocol decreed they could not be kept, but Emily only once confessed to a pang over the presents from the Prince of Oude in Cawnpore:

> He had had two diamond combs made on purpose for F and me, mounted in an European fashion . . . there were also two lovely pairs of earrings, a single uncut emerald drop, with one large diamond at the top . . . This is the first time the presents have excited my cupidity. Not the combs–I am grown too old for a comb; but those emerald earrings!

She contented herself with drawing these dazzling princes. In Shalimar she wrote:

> Shere Singh came to my tent to sit for his picture–such a gorgeous figure! All over diamonds and emeralds; and as it was a first private visit he brought a bag of rupees which he waved round and threw on the ground, and of which it is indelicate to take the least notice.

The Eden sisters saw a much harsher world during their long tour to the north-west. They travelled in a ten-mile-long cavalcade of some splendour, but Emily never got used to camping:

> The first evening of tents, I must say, was more uncomfortable than I had ever fancied. Everybody kept saying 'What a magnificent camp' and I thought I never had seen such squalid, melancholy discomfort.

In fact, George, Emily and Fanny had a tent each, with a fourth to make it a private square and covered passages linking one to another. Each had a bedroom, dressing-room and sitting-room, and a red cloth wall enclosed the whole thing, but to Emily 'it feels *open-airish* and unsafe'. In some camps the neigh-

Emily Eden went to India with her sister Fanny and her brother. He was governor general so they moved in the world of nawabs and maharajahs. A talented artist, Emily drew her impressions for posterity, including this picture of Shere Singh.

ing of the cavalry horses disturbed her, and she claimed the infantry regiment had got 'a mad drummer' who started drumming at dawn and stopped at dusk. Even when their tents withstood a thunderstorm she said ungratefully, 'I shall be glad to be settled at Simla.'

It is inevitable that women of Emily and Fanny Eden's background should display some inflexible prejudices. They were particularly annoyed by the omnipresence of large, exuberant Mrs Fanny Parkes, an indefatigable traveller who had the nerve to foist herself on the Governor-General's encampment. Janet Dunbar (in her book *Golden Interlude*) quotes a letter Fanny Eden wrote to Eleanor Grosvenor:

> We are rather oppressed just now by a lady, Mrs Parkes, who insists on belonging to our camp. She has succeeded in proving that the Governor-General's power is but a name. She has a husband who always goes mad in the cold season, so she says it is her duty to herself to leave him and travel about. She has been a beauty and has remains of it and is abundantly fat and lively. At Benares, where we fell in with her, she informed us she was an independent woman and was going to travel to Simla by herself–which sounded very independent indeed.

Irritating though Mrs Parkes may have been, she was one of the few Englishwomen with a wide knowledge of native customs and who took the trouble to learn Hindustani, and she makes a virtuous contrast to Emily who wrote on Christmas Day, 1837:

> I am particularly *Indianly* low today. There is such a horrid mixture of sights and sounds for Christmas . . . Somehow a detestation of the Hindustani language, sounding all round us, came over me in a very inexplicable manner.

Yet colour had less significance for her than many of the resident British community:

> . . . the sepoys seem to be much finer soldiers than our people, partly from being so tall and upright; and then I am convinced that brown is the natural colour for a man–black and white are unnatural deviations and look shocking. I am quite ashamed of our white skins.

Like so many memsahibs before her, Emily Eden found Simla highly congenial after the heat and dust of the plains. It was, after all, reassuringly like England–the return to which was the Holy Grail of all Emily's Indian experience. There was 'an English cuckoo talking English' in Simla, and 'beautiful walks like English shrubberies cut on all sides of the hills'. 'Good,' she wrote, 'I see this is to be the best part of India.'

If Emily Eden waited impatiently to quit India, Honoria Lawrence chafed at the home leaves with her two sons which parted her from it and from the husband she adored. She was married to Sir Henry Lawrence, the first British Ruler of the Punjab and a practical philanthropist of great vision. It was a true love affair and an equal partnership. Unlike Emily Eden, she was a born comrade for the wild camp-life of their early days in India. Only three months married, they trekked across country by buggy and doolie from Revelgunj to Gorakhpur. They could only travel from dusk to dawn because of the heat, joggling along at five miles an hour over cart-tracks submerged by the last of the monsoon rains. Honoria had an irrepressibly optimistic attitude to discomfort, revelling in the beauty of her surroundings and 'sleeping with such profoundness as I never remember at home'. Henry bore this out in their shared journal:

> . . . at 11 p.m. while you are snoring like a young rhinoceros, I again take up the book to testify how good a traveller you are, how courageous by land and water, how gentle and forebearing to your cross husband.

These silhouettes of Henry and Honoria Laurence were 'cut' in Lahore in 1852 by Mrs Kate Hill.

But away from the open-air life and intimacy and settled in Henry's station in Gorakhpur, Honoria found her wifely obligations much more difficult. Emily Eden managed to mask her indifference to the social duties by which most memsahibs made their contribution, but Honoria could not conceal her impatience: 'I'd rather be a kitten and cry mew than pass my time in such superficial intercourse.' She was oppressed by the multitude of servants and the lack of privacy, and feared acquiring the overbearing manner that was sadly identified with the resident British.

> The whole system is very hurtful to one's mind. You have your servants at so much a month and you have no further concern with them . . . It is all very free from care, but tends to make one inconsiderate.

Even her beloved Henry seemed to have acquired the prevalent habit and earns a rebuke–'you, dearest, scarcely ever address a native without an abusive epithet–even when you are not angry.' Moving in the highest social circles, Emily Eden observes the same thing, though a trifle snobbishly:

> Even now it is very painful to hear the way in which even some of the best Europeans speak to those Rajpoot princes, who, though we have conquered them, still are considered as kings by their subjects, and who look like high caste people.

In 1843 Henry Lawrence was appointed British Resident in Nepal: an empire where no white woman was officially allowed. Typically, Henry circumvented the problem, the Nepalese turned a blind eye and Honoria was permitted to join him. By this time they had a five-year-old son and with him and the bearers Honoria travelled alone to the Gurkha capital, attributing her safety to 'the spell of the English name'. In Oudh a Mohammedan pitched her a scarlet and white tent 'with gilt pinnacles to the poles'. Beautiful as it was, it was full of gaps ('*open-airish*' as Emily Eden would have said) but Honoria was too tired to care, simply enjoying 'glimpses of diamond stars'.

Life in the mountain kingdom was circumscribed: 'We are completely secluded, not only by the jealous policy of the Nepal government but by the miasma afloat in the belt of Terai forests that surrounds the lower hills'. But Honoria was happiest when secluded: the Lawrences rode together, wrote together, discussed politics and finally produced another son–'The first Christian infant born in Nepal.'

Moving from post to post was a recurrent feature of an Indian career. Since the eccentric Henry Lawrence was something of a puzzle to his superiors he was frequently moved on. Mrs Flora Annie Steel (1847–1929), joint author of *The Complete Indian Housekeeper and Cook*, gives us some idea of what a circus these journeys must have been:

> The following is a list showing the way in which the property of a family, consisting of a lady, three or four children, and an English nurse, might be packed and loaded:
>
> 1st camel load:
> Two large trunks and two smaller ones with clothing.
> 2nd camel load:
> One large trunk containing children's clothing, plate chest, three bags, and one bonnet-box.
> 3rd camel load:
> Three boxes of books, one box containing folding chairs, light tin box with clothing.
> 4th camel load:
> Four cases of stores, four cane chairs, saddlestand, mackintosh sheets.
> 5th camel load:
> One chest of drawers, two iron cots, tea table, pans for washing up.
> 6th camel load:
> Second chest of drawers, screen, lamps, lanterns, hanging wardrobes.
> 7th camel load:
> Two boxes containing house linen, two casks containing ornaments, ice-pails, door mats.
> 8th camel load:
> Three casks of crockery, another cask containing ornaments, filter, pardah [purdah] bamboos, tennis poles.
> 9th camel load:
> Hot case, milk safe, baby's tub and stand, sewing-machine, fender and irons, water cans, pitchers.

A simple form of palanquin was employed to carry the ladies as they travelled east.

10th camel load:
Three boxes containing saddlery, kitchen utensils, carpets.
11th camel load:
Two boxes containing drawing room sundries, servants' coats, iron bath, cheval glass, plate basket.

Or the above articles could be loaded on four country carts, each with three or four bullocks for up hill journey ... A piano, where carts can be used, requires a cart to itself, and should be swung to avoid being injured by jolting. If the road is only a camel road, the piano must be carried by coolies, of whom fourteen or sixteen will be needed ... When a march is made by stages, and one's own cows accompany, these latter should start, after being milked, the night before the family.

But Honoria, away from all this with her boys in England, longed only to be back. Her absence confirmed her passion for India–*her* India, with its freedom and escape from the conventions. When Henry, bitterly at odds with the rest of his administration over Punjabi policy, resigned in 1852, he was posted as Resident in Rajputana. To him it seemed like exile; to Honoria, hurrying back, it meant contentment. As in Nepal, she had Henry to herself. The Residency at Mount Abn in the Aravalli Range was perched high on a rock above a lake, where Honoria found peace:

I like to watch the kites sailing in circles and the busy little swallows skimming among them unmolested. Then we have a lovely little humming bird that hovers like a butterfly over a flower, plunges in its long slender beak and sucks the honey. Altogether there is great happiness here.

There she died in 1854, aged forty-five, worn out by India.

Henry Lawrence lived another three and a half years until the siege of Lucknow. He was fatally wounded when the Residency was subjected to a storm of shot and shell. Both gave their lives for the Empire, Honoria playing an active contributory part in her husband's career.

The author of the indispensable handbook for memsahibs quoted earlier did more than contribute to her husband's career in India, she created one of her own. Flora Annie Steel travelled to India aged twenty in 1868 as the bride of Henry Steel, an officer of the Indian Civil Service. She was a supremely energetic woman; as a child her recurrent cry had been, 'I can do that,' and her brother declared that her energy would be a upas tree that would overshadow her whole life. She embraced the challenge of life in India with optimism and enthusiasm. In her frank autobiography, *The Garden of Fidelity*, she described how she, like Eliza Fay, landed through the crashing surf at Madras:

> It was exhilarating. Something quite new; something that held all possibilities. A boat that had not a nail in it; a dark-skinned boatman with no clothes on . . . a surf such as I had never seen before, thundering on yellow sands.

She endured, like so many before her, the tragic loss of her first child, but even that misery did not dim for long her capacity to immerse herself in new and demanding activities. When her

Flora Annie Steel is seen here before she sailed for India, aged 20, the bride of an officer in the ICS. Unlike most Raj ladies, Flora learnt the language and was an expert on India. She became a well-known novelist and her household compendium was a primer for the ladies of the Fishing Fleet.

husband was transferred to Dalhousie and called upon to make an extensive report, he was weak from fever, so Flora took over his duties:

> It was my first experience of a Government office, and it left me a confirmed Individualist for the rest of my life. I saw clearly that everything–order, method, punctuality, efficiency–depended upon one individuality only. So I gripped the fact, to which I have held ever since, that the best form of Government is a beneficent Autocracy. Democracy went by the board as a thing of Mediocrity, the Apotheosis of Bureaucracy. So the files were rearranged; facts disclosed themselves during the process; and the report was, I believe, considered exhaustive. But to me, recovering as I was from a knock-down blow, it opened up hitherto undreamt-of chambers of thoughts as to the how and the why of many Governmental shibboleths.

In addition, she played the harmonium in church, ran the Christmas Eve Ball, and produced a play for the New Year. In pursuit of props and settings, Flora found '. . . there is hardly anything which you cannot get in an Indian bazaar, provided you know the proper name for it'. Accordingly, she learnt the language properly, not just the domestic patois used by most Raj ladies. Happily she soon gave birth to a second child, a daughter, who survived. 'I felt supreme bliss in gazing at her infantile ugliness,' said Flora–then, afraid of a lapse into sentimentality, continued more characteristically, 'I felt something had been achieved.'

There was more to achieve, of course, given her monumental energy. Alone among Englishwomen married to officials in India, Flora became deeply involved in the lives of the Indians. When Henry was posted to Kasur, a sub-division of the Lahore district, she set herself up as a doctor, despite a lack of training: 'Looking back I rather wondered at my own self-confidence, or rather cheek, in using quite dangerous drugs.' But her first big case was a providential success. She defied local custom in her treatment of puerperal fever and the patient recovered– 'After that if I had chosen to order the painting a patient pea-green it would have been done.'

Her 'cheek' carried her next into the field of education. Accompanying her husband on his inspection of schools, she decided to instigate bi-weekly classes in English which worked very well until she was disconcerted by the differences between East and West. She was surprised to discover that the reason one of her pupils ('a nice boy of about thirteen') was delivering poor work was because he was distraught about his sick baby, of whom the mother was aged twelve. It made her reconsider the wisdom of educating India on Western lines:

> But give an instant's thought to the poor lad who was trying

to mix up English grammar with fatherhood and will there not be a heart whole condemnation of trying to put new wine into old bottles?

Early in her Indian career Flora came up against authority, had a vigorous skirmish, and won, thereby establishing the pattern of her relationship with the Government in India. The Prince of Wales was coming out to Lahore and a large standing camp was erected with miles of tents, flower beds of chrysanthemum shoots and palm trees. Marquees were designated as the royal drawing-room, dining-room etc, and Flora cleverly offered her grand piano, seeing it as a means of getting it tuned at last.

So, knowing the Government official in charge of the camp, I offered the use of the instrument for the drawing-room; for, of course, but for this suggestion, a piano would have been absolutely out of reach; there was none for hire nearer than Calcutta. The offer was gratefully accepted, and from our own tents, which we had pitched under some trees hard by, as my husband loathed constant society, we could hear it being thrummed upon with vigour. Now those who used the Government tents in the standing camp were charged ten rupees a day to cover the expenses of roads, lighting, sanitation, and lodging. We had none of these things, so I was indignant at being charged for them, and protested. Quite a wordy war ensued which ended by my husband sending in a bill of sixteen rupees a day–the usual charge–for the use of the piano. This abjectly foolish little episode lingers in my memory . . . as an excellent example of the strange niggardliness of Government which has done more to lower the prestige of our rule in India than anything else.

Lady travellers in India rarely seem to have disguised themselves in native dress. Emily Eden refers to her dusty brown bonnet with veil, and a cloak which she once wore over a dressing gown. Lady Curzon wore a topee when hunting, but this was presumably for practical reasons rather than to disguise herself as a hunter. In fact, eleven different types of topee were illustrated in Rural Life in Bengal *only one of which we should call by that name today. Strangely enough, the author describes the 'normal' topee as 'distinguished for nothing but its unmitigated tastelessness and vulgarity'. Fanny Bullock also wore a topee on her bicycle trips.*

Next, Flora took it upon herself to design a municipal hall for Kasur. The local committee was enchanted by her plans, which included an arch sixteen feet wide, but the Department of Public Works rejected her sketch 'and presented in its stead a very creditable drawing of a Swiss Chalet. Anything more unsuitable could scarcely have been devised.' Her design was not entirely architecturally practicable, but the municipal committee went ahead and it was completed. Then came devastating rains, and Flora feared for the safety of her arch. However, her reputation was to be enhanced on two levels. There had been a long drought, and twelve Hindu *yogis* and twelve Mohammedan *fakirs* sat naked in the sun without food or water for twenty-four hours to pray for rain. Flora pointed out that it might be wise to qualify the request with some limiting adjective 'such as a *little* rain, *enough* rain or *sufficient* rain'. She was being facetious, but when the rain fell it was almost twice the annual rainfall in eight hours, and her joke was taken as clear evidence of her foreknowledge. What was more, the arch survived.

Local respect for her powers was so great that she was invited to become a Begum, to control a private kingdom and to arbitrate over her people independently of outside laws. It was a serious temptation to Flora ('What a tyrant I should have been! What a thorn in the side of any self-respecting British government.') but she turned it down on the grounds that India was inimical to her husband's health and they could never make a long-term commitment. Henry may have seen Flora's abrasive relations with his employers as inimical to his career, but he never interfered with her ebullient schemes. When their daughter was sent to school in England, Flora did not divide her time between husband and child, as so many Anglo-Indian mothers did; she stayed with Henry. It must have been a difficult choice, for the opening of the Suez Canal in 1869 had literally opened up the lives of the memsahibs. Flora was now part of a new generation who could commute to and fro on annual leaves and return for school holidays, for the sailing time from Europe to India was halved to three weeks. But Henry's health was poor and Flora saw it as incumbent on her to take over his duties whenever he was unable.

Apart from these labours, she somehow managed to achieve real progress in social reform for the women of India. Never a militant, she felt fiery feminism would be counter-productive, and attacked the problem from the root by strongly advocating the education of women. As usual, her views brought her into conflict with the authorities. She opened a school for girls in Kasur in 1874; by 1884 she had bullied the government into appointing her the first inspectress of girls' schools, and from 1885 to 1888 she served on the Provincial Education Board.

In addition to all this, Flora somehow found time to write two books before her husband's retirement. *The Complete Indian Cook and Housekeeper* became a positive primer for the Fishing Fleet–no young woman planning to run a home in India could afford to ignore its very practical instruction.

It was much more of a wrench for Flora than for Henry when the time came to leave India and the women she had influenced:

But the time was fast approaching when my husband was to retire. He had always disliked Government service, and I fear my many tussles with it had not made him like it the more. But I had always been successful with my own work. Over 20,000 girls passed through my hands on this my last tour, and I really do not think I had made an enemy amongst the women.

Nor had I antagonised the men. At any rate I was asked to nominate my successor: which I did.

My last act on the Educational Board was to promise to write a primer on Hygiene for the girls' Middle-School examination which was to take the place of the perfectly useless euclid.

Then came the good-byes to my own particular schools.

The indomitable Flora Annie Steel in later life.

> Doubtless we wept a good deal, but my last recollection was an extremely cheerful one. A crowd of some three hundred veiled women on the platform of the railway station, far too excited over the strangeness of their own behaviour, to think even of tears!

She did not leave for ever. In 1894 she returned to her beloved Kasur to prepare her novel of the Indian Mutiny. *On The Face of The Waters* won her recognition: she became famous for her capacity to recreate the Indian scene. Her research was impeccable, but it was her unconscious assimilation of scenes and sensations that gave her book its potent reality.

EM Forster, who was beguiled by but critical of the vigorous Eliza Fay, had a truer admiration for women who responded to mysticism, as manifested by his characterization of Mrs Moore in *A Passage to India*. His foreword to *Flowers and Elephants* (1927) by Constance Sitwell categorizes her as a woman who could feel and wonder at the soul of India. By no means all the Raj ladies dealt in Western practicalities only: there were visionary dreamers among them. Constance Sitwell's vivid writing could at first glance be mistaken for a slightly breathless account by a member of the Fishing Fleet who stayed with her brother in India–she details all the expected activities. She visited Bombay and the Taj Mahal; she went on an elephant drive; she met maharajahs; she explored bazaars; she chatted in clubs; she turned down a few proposals. But the book is more complex than that. She laughs at herself for her 'priggish' visions, yet her perception is of another reality:

> After riding some distance through green glooms the path brought us out on to the side of a hill, and there–through the straight rough trunks of gigantic deodars–I saw, with a soft inner shock, distant shapes, mightily ranged, the shining Himalayas. The sight struck me with a kind of terror, those mountains seemed wrought upon a different scale from anything else on earth or in the experience of human kind. 'And yet there are men living near those snows,' I thought, 'pilgrims, and holy men in caves, who have chosen that way of life.'
>
> 'Think of the hermits–the rishis living up there with their austere and solemn joys,' I said to Richard rather priggishly, pointing to the mountains with my riding-whip.
>
> 'Joys!' he laughed. 'Humph! What joys can there be up there in the cold? Neither joy nor use, to my mind.'
>
> And he went on to ask me whether I thought *I* should find up there the peace they talked of; I told him I wasn't made of such heroic stuff and could not do without earthly delights, but that the rare people I was thinking of, who might belong to any race or any religion, existed on a different level and had a different sense of reality. But we didn't argue for long; he wouldn't agree that there were other joys–far more living and exultant–than ours.

At the end of the book, when she is back in England contemplating her unsettling impressions of India, she finds a philosophical peace herself:

> The disquiet of the past months fell away from me. I knew there was permanence: I felt reality. A bubble of eternity had risen through time and held me for an instant in its shining peace. 'I shall find them again,' I said to myself, 'the flowers and jungles and innocent huge beasts. I shall find them where the pattern of these things eternally dwells.'

Agnes Huddleston and her husband, George, both of whom came from families who regarded India as their heritage, were also a couple whose outward conventionality may have masked an unusual sensitivity to Eastern spirituality. His first novel *The White Fakir, a tale of the Mystical East* (1932) must have been an unexpected consummation of twenty years of a typical career in the Indian Railways. The foreword tells us 'During my time in India I heard more than once of a British woman who was living the life of an ascetic in the hills.' The novel is about Jean Preston, who left her husband when they were living in India to wander in the hills 'where she became a devotee of Krishna', a choice which George Huddleston obviously admires. His second book *Kissed by the Sun* is dedicated to Agnes 'in memory of our golden years'. Its heroine is the half-white half-Indian Molly, who returns to India after her English education and, like Jean Preston, discovers a mystical 'golden streak of glory'. She meets a childhood Indian friend Mahomet and forms a spiritual partnership in which sexual love has no part:

> That night, beneath the Eastern stars, which seemed to her to shine with greater brightness than ever before, Molly lay awake on the warm earth under the shadow of a feather-leaved tamarind tree. By her side slept Mahomet. Little did she realize how happily he was dreaming until she heard him murmur, 'Love is Paradise'.
>
> Then, as her heart responded, he awoke.
>
> 'What have you been thinking of?' she asked, though she knew very well that his thoughts invariably ran on but one theme. It had become an obsession. "I have been dreaming of love, and will tell you of the vision that came to me in my sleep. I saw an unfathomable ocean, as illimitable as the firmament above and as free as the air we breathe. I learnt that all who desire happiness may enter its joyous portals; all are welcome to its sweet embrace. No one is questioned, no one is ever rejected; it is full of sunshine. I learnt, once again, that love was the only Paradise on earth, and the only way to heaven.'
>
> 'A wonderful truth; but have we not already found that out for ourselves?' '*We* have, but others stand aloof. Is it not strange that the world hesitates on the brink of that glorious ocean, preferring to quarrel and wrangle; brother fighting brother, filled with jealousy, envy, malice, and every other prompting of Shaitan, instead of walking into peace and happiness?'

It was symbolic that a woman should have opened up the lives of the ladies of India—the Empress Eugenie of France who, in November 1869, formally opened the Suez Canal, an act which halved the sailing time from Europe to India to three weeks. This made it possible to effectively 'commute' to and fro on annual leaves, and to send children to boarding school in England without the feeling that one was saying goodbye to them for ever. From the 1870s onwards, the lives of the reasonably well-to-do ladies of the raj became almost a pleasure.

One wonders if these were the terms in which the Huddlestons conversed and it is an intriguing counterpoint to the life that they led in Raj society. Rail was held in esteem, so they were well placed in the social pecking order. Agnes lived in pleasant bungalows with a full complement of servants; she travelled with her husband, or led a gay social life while he was away attending to time-tables and tracks. Her way of life was encapsulated in her scrap-books and photograph albums, and through them we can glimpse her for a period of about twenty years, from 1893 when she was twenty-seven years old until the outbreak of the 1914–1918 war when she returned home leaving India for ever.

The Huddlestons, part of whose Indian scrapbook appears on the following pages, had ancestors who became pillars of the Indian establishment, amongst them the Lawrences. One Huddleston was awarded the Victoria Cross while serving with the Ghurkas.

Agnes, who compiled the scrapbook, was the daughter of a magistrate in India. Her husband George wrote in his family book, The Huddlestons by a Huddleston for the Huddlestons *that 'she was fond of games and sport. She was devoted also to dancing and music; sang solos in Calcutta Cathedral, often took leading parts in musical comedies and at concerts and parties. She was in great requisition both in Calcutta and up country.'*

The centre of her life was the Club and other sources of entertainment like the racecourse, with its regular events like the Ladies' Paperchase Cup. There was also polo, which, along with pig-sticking and tiger hunting, was one of the most prestigious sports and one in which—sometimes—the ladies partook.

The greatest social event of their early years was unquestionably the Coronation Durbar in Delhi, organised by the Viceroy, Lord Curzon, to mark Edward VII's accession. They arrived in Delhi several days in advance of the ceremony. On the night before the Durbar the Huddlestons were at the Bengal Camp Dinner—menu in French—and they then joined the 160,000 guests in the giant arena which Curzon built especially for the one-day event on January 1st, 1903. By January 6th, the Huddlestons were dancing at the magnificent state ball, also at Delhi (which was not yet the centre of government). Later, when the Mintos succeeded the Curzons, the Huddlestons were invited to meet the new Viceroy, the invitation coming from Lord Kitchener himself, who by his wiles had ousted Curzon from power.

Life, as revealed in the papers of Agnes and George, is a far from serious business. The attitudes are conventional, and one might safely assume that Agnes lived the life she might have lived had their address been Surrey and not Simla. Even Agnes' attitude to the Indians appears absolutely conventional, if we take it at its face value.

And yet . . . and yet. Were the Huddlestons really as conventional members of the raj quartet as the scrapbook would lead one to believe? The evidence against is to be found in two novels which George wrote on his return to England.

GRAMMAR SCHOOL
MODEL YACHTING CLUB.
WILL HOLD A REGATTA ON SATURDAY NEXT
(WEATHER PERMITTING)
The President Requests the Company
of Mr Huddleston & &
PARK POND 3
P.T.O.
TIME 2.30

Lord & Lady Irwin

request the pleasure of

Colonel C. Huddleston's

Company at Luncheon

on Friday the 6th February

at 1.40 o'Clock

R.S.V.P.
to the A.D.C. in waiting

This card must be shown to secure admittance to the Durbar Amphitheatre.

Delhi Coronation Durbar

1st January 1903.

Admit Mr Huddleston

to Block II No. 131

H S Barnes

Officers in uniform "Full Dress."
Others "Morning Dress."

Foreign Secretary.

CORONATION DURBAR,

DELHI,

1st JANUARY 1903.

Speech delivered by
His Excellency The Viceroy,
Lord Curzon, G.M.S.I., G.M.I.E.

The Aide de Camp in waiting is commanded by

His Excellency The Viceroy

to invite

Mr Sw. Huddleston

to a Ball on Tuesday

the 6th of January 1903 at 9.30 o'Clock

DIWAN-I-AM.   DELHI FORT.

MENU

MINTO FANCY FÊTE,
PRINCES RESTAURANT
5th FEBRUARY 1903.

1st: M. dely
good.

Diner.

Les Huitres.

Tortue Claire.

Tranches de Saumon d'Ecosse, Bearnaise.

Faisans Hongrois Perigord.

Punch à la Val de Rue.

Selle de Pre-sale a la Broche.
Dinde farci.

Salsifis au beurre fondu.

Peches Nesselrode.

Canapes Forestiere.

Dessert.

Bombe Tosca.

Café.

This is the ship
Whereon we met;
And so did the Sea & the Sky
And yet.
'Twas fair with you.
"Dear-sye".
This is the chair
I loved to see
On which you sat
Then stamped on one !
Oh! Why? 
This is the tear
I shed with a sigh
And I stammered a last.
Bow - a long good bye.
And a cry!

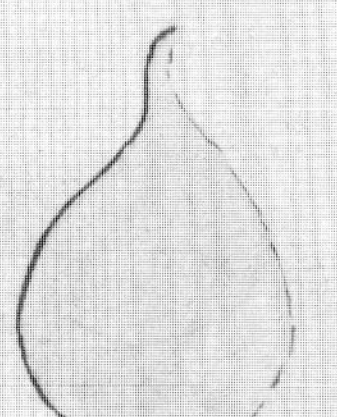

This is the end
Of my tale of woe;
You'll finish the bottle
Tomorrow I know!
Then die.

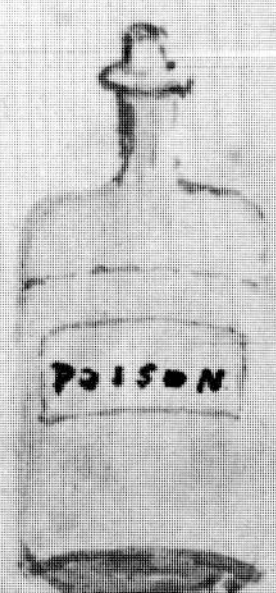

T Komyns Carr.
Arthurs Club.
London.

POISON

CHAPTER 7

MASQUERADERS

This oil painting of James Silk Buckingham and his wife Elizabeth now hangs in the Royal Geographical Society's premises in London. In his autobiography, Buckingham tells how his wife and his 3-year-old daughter joined him (the year was 1811) on a voyage to the East. In Smyrna he took the two of them to visit the Governor's harem, where a Turkish lady expressed surprise 'at the slender waist of my wife, still more [so] when informed that she was the mother of the child who accompanied her. She could not comprehend how the human figure could be compressed into such compass and asked to be permitted to examine the dress . . . On arriving at the stays, and seeing the manner in which it was tightly laced, her wonder was at the climax . . . Still greater was her surprise to learn that a slender figure was regarded as a feminine trait of beauty.'

As to the painting, Buckingham notes that: 'So many amusing anecdotes to which my being dressed in the Turkish manner had given rise, induced the artist, Mr Jukes, to request that I would sit to him for my picture.'

Disguise was often a more complex matter than a whim or a vanity of the woman traveller. The eighteenth- and nineteenth-century aristocrats who had the means and inclination to go abroad came from an unselfconscious social tradition of 'dressing-up' for masquerades and costume balls. But their transformation on their travels was usually more than mere sartorial flamboyance. There were obvious climatic and practical advantages in adopting native dress. They could raise or lower their status more recognizably when they presented it in terms of local costume, although this could be a trap for the unwary! There was often a romantic element–some women adopted their new dress to please indigenous lovers or husbands. And, of course, to adopt the costume of a country is to pay it a graceful compliment.

Thorough-going transvestism among early women travellers was not as common as might be thought. Those that did adopt male attire permanently were undoubtedly influenced by more than practical thinking, and were expressing a deep-seated dissatisfaction with the feminine predicament. Their adopted dress seems to have had a notable effect on their concept of themselves.

Many Victorian travellers refused to compromise over what they wore and made little or no concession to climate or custom. They clung to uncomfortable, impracticable clothing in order to maintain their own concept of respectability, or invented subtle modifications that did not undermine the contemporary notion of 'femininity'.

Real disguise, as opposed to 'dressing-up', was a more serious matter, adopted by those who could not reveal their identity or their nationality for political reasons. These women had to be free to observe, yet be unobserved–not just a vindication of wearing foreign clothes, but perhaps a definition of the best kind of traveller.

Lady Mary Wortley Montagu (1689–1762) belonged to the

Lady Mary Wortley Montagu had her portrait painted in Arab costume but underneath it all she continued to wear the ubiquitous stays.

group of aristocrats who found it delightfully easy to flaunt flamboyantly in costume abroad. Self-educated, having had the run of her father's library (he was the Duke of Kingston), her friends included Alexander Pope and John Gay. With her opinionated and daring manner, she became famous throughout Europe for her 'Turkish Embassy' letters, written when her husband was posted to Turkey as British Ambassador in 1716. Even the preparations for her departure had a decidedly theatrical air. She bought a black wig which she maintained would serve as a comfortable and warm head-dress; a dashing tricorne hat and a riding-habit modelled after the man's fashion. However, it was what lay beneath that most intrigued the ladies in the Turkish baths at Istanbul: 'I was at last forced . . . to show them my stays which satisfied 'em very well, for I saw they believed I was so locked up in that machine that it was not in my own power to open it, which contrivance they attributed to my husband.'

Vanity was a powerful inducement to adopt a flattering foreign costume. Lady Mary wrote to her sister in minute detail about her fetching new appearance:

The first piece of my dress is a pair of drawers, very full, that reach to my shoes, and conceal the legs more modestly than your petticoats. They are of a thin rose-coloured damask, brocaded with silver flowers, my shoes of white kid leather,

embroidered with gold. Over this hangs my smock, of a fine white silk gauze, edged with embroidery. This smock has wide sleeves hanging half-way down the arm, and is closed at the neck with a diamond button; but the shape and colour of the bosom very well to be distinguished through it. The *antery* is a waistcoat, made close to the shape of white and gold damask ... My *caftan*, of the same stuff, with my drawers, is a robe exactly fitted to my shape, and reaching to my feet, with very long, straight falling sleeves. Over this is the girdle of about four fingers broad, which all that can afford have entirely of diamonds or other precious stones ... The *Curdee* is a loose robe they throw off or put on according to the weather, being of a rich brocade (mine is green and gold), either lined with ermine or sables ... The head-dress is composed of a cap, called *talpock*, which is in winter of fine velvet embroidered with pearls or diamonds, and in summer of a light shining silver stuff. This is fixed on one side of the head ...

She also took the very sensible precaution of having her portrait painted for posterity to admire the whole fetching effect.

Lady Hester Stanhope (1776–1863) was the eccentric daughter of the third Earl of Stanhope and the clever niece of Prime Minister William Pitt. She became his hostess and most trusted confidante. He said of her, 'I let her do as she pleases;

'We all mean to dress in future as Turks', wrote Lady Hester Stanhope on her way to Alexandria. She believed Asiatic dress, as she called it, suited her better than anything else. It certainly contributed to her reputation for eccentricity and the English travellers who called at her eastern home always felt it necessary to give her description in some detail.

for if she were resolved to cheat the devil she could do it.' To which Hester Stanhope added, 'And so I could.' Like Lady Mary Wortley Montagu, she was always unconventional and, by virtue of her position, able to be untrammelled by social tradition. As a result, though, she had no female friends–which may account in some measure for the alacrity with which she adopted male dress on her travels. An unrequited passion for Lord Granville Leveson-Gower, and the loss of her status when Pitt died, drove her abroad in 1810, and poverty finally kept her there. Accompanied by two debonair young men and her personal physician, Dr Meryon, who considered himself her Boswell, she was shipwrecked on the way to Alexandria, losing all her possessions. She immediately took to wearing Turkish men's costume, knowing how well it would suit her rangy figure: 'We all mean to dress in future as Turks. I assure you that if ever I looked well in anything it is in Asiatic dress.'

James Silk Buckingham, who stayed for nine days at Lady Hester Stanhope's winter home near Sidon in 1816 (and dedicated to her his *Travels in Mesopotamia 1827*), sought to explain that 'subject of wonder'–why Lady Hester should wear the dress of a Turkish Effendi or private gentleman.

> The wonder will cease, however, when the reasons which influenced this choice are explained. Had she retained the dress of an English lady, she could never have ventured into the open air, even for the purpose of exercise, without attracting a crowd of peasantry, and others, to witness such a curiosity as anyone so apparelled could not fail to be considered in that country, and this would be a perpetual impediment to all her movements abroad. Had she adopted the dress of a Turkish lady, she could never have ventured out except in the ample garments worn by these . . . The dress of an English gentleman [he labours on] would be liable to still stronger objections, though of another nature; so that the Turkish male dress appeared the only one that could be adopted with delicacy and advantage combined . . . [for] it conceals the whole figure and person of the wearer . . . nothing can be more consistent with the most feminine delicacy . . . so that the choice was wise and prudent and in every other respect quite unexceptionable.

Mrs Fry, Lady Hester's maid, took great exception to the idea of dressing in men's clothes. But her mistress overruled her, pointing out the disadvantages of going permanently veiled, as local taboos demanded of women. Reluctantly Mrs Fry capitulated. She was not so steeped in the sartorial exhibitionism that came naturally to the English upper classes.

Jane Digby (1807–1881) came from that tradition, but her transformation into a Bedouin wife was less marked by vanity than the costume changes of these predecessors. A legendary beauty, her appearance seems to have mattered very little to

Stays again–this time drawn by a cartoonist who wanted to shock his readers at the irregular life of Jane Digby on the Continent.

She was witty, well-read and worldly-wise, but Lady Jane Digby's love life was distinctly complex, and she moved slowly but surely eastwards until she found the real passion of her life in the Bedouin tents with a Sheik.

her, and the drama of her life may have assuaged any desire to show off. She changed husbands and lovers almost as often as her clothes–the list of her marriages reads, as she put it, 'like a naughty *Almanach de Gotha*'. Before she was seventeen her marriage was arranged to Lord Ellenborough, but it ended in the scandal of a divorce heard in the House of Lords. Marriages to Baron Venningen, Count Theotoky and Sheik Abdul Medjuel El Mezrab followed, involving a tally of elopements, a duel and a further divorce. Jane spent thirty years with Medjuel, and is described as sartorially the simplest of wives, 'wearing one blue garment, her beautiful hair in two long plaits down to the ground, milking the camels, serving her husband'. This approving vignette was written by Isobel Burton, wife of the famous Orientalist, Richard Burton, who cannot, however, resist a moralistic side-swipe about Jane's earlier appearance and lifestyle: 'When I first saw her in Damascus . . . she blackened her eyes with kohl and lived in a curiously untidy manner.'

Byron's grand-daughter, Lady Anne Blunt, had the strongest reason for travelling–she had to keep an eye on her amorous husband Wilfrid. So, if he wore disguise, she must too. In European clothes he said he felt 'naked' and from their house near Cairo they would travel wrapped in Bedouin cloaks and the yellow fellah or native turban–equally good as helmet, bandage, girdle or pillow. Here she is seen with her horse Kassida, before the Blunts returned to England to found the famous Arab stud. But after her eastern experiences, Lady Anne thought it wrong to be without a hat or turban even in her bedroom. 'Thus in bed she would wear a small fishing hat and a mackintosh' instead of a nightdress, in the words of her son-in-law, dressed 'as though for the southwest gale in the channel.' Her husband continued to wear Arab outfit as must his guests, so 'dress up for dinner' acquired a new meaning at his house. There is splendid vignette of Churchill in 1915, sitting at table with Blunt, Belloc, and others, lecturing them on the errors of the War Office–all dressed as Arabs.

This is borne out–in a less narrow-minded way–by Anne Blunt who was travelling in Damascus at the same period. Stoic about the philanderings of her poet-explorer husband Wilfrid Scawen Blunt, she was the last person to be condemnatory about 'untidy' morals–indeed, she was a great admirer of the seventy-year-old Jane Digby El Mezrab. But she, too, thought it a shame to adopt the worst Arab fashions of kohl and black hair-dye. Not that the Blunts proved to have impeccable instincts on the subject of disguise. Their propensity for travelling in ragged clothes the better to blend with the Arabs brought its own problems. It disguised them too well: the Persians of Dizful mistook them for Bedouin outcasts. Hindered in her journey by the 'foolish questions' of the Persian bureaucrats of that 'tiresome city', Anne Blunt rolled up her Bedouin sleeves to reveal her white skin–to general amazement. Perhaps they should have paid attention to Richard Burton. 'Throughout the East,' he wrote, 'a badly dressed man is a pauper, and as in England, a pauper is a scoundrel.'

Conversely–but equally mistakenly–Lady Hester Stanhope grabbed indiscriminately at gorgeous apparel without attempting to understand the etiquette of Turkish dress. Delighting in her new masculine impersonation–which released an already marked capacity to take her pleasures in her own way–she arrayed herself in the eye-catching court dress of a Tunisian Bey. When she visited Mehemet Ali at Usbekiah Palace she wore purple and gold pantaloons, her girdle and turban of the finest cashmere shawls. The Pashahik of Cairo may well have found it amusing to receive his angular blue-eyed guest in her costume of the Barbary States!

Eventually, though, her knowledge of Syrian costume tradition became encyclopaedic, and she was then typically impatient at the ignorance of others. Poor Dr Meryon's wife committed a major gaffe. Hester decked her in a gold brocade cloak and finely embroidered turban before entertaining her to one of her interminable hookah-smoking, monologuing 'conversations'. Mrs Meryon removed the clothes before she left, imagining she had been part of some childish dressing-up game. Hester was furious: tradition demanded Mrs Meryon should thank her hostess and leave wearing the clothes. The days of masquerades had been left far behind: her clothes, to her, were what made her an indigenous part of Syria.

Transvestism among women travellers mostly had its roots in practicality. Lady Hester never set out to pass herself off as a man: her arrogance in refusing to wear the veil, coupled with her male costume, led to her being mistaken for a beardless boy. Her paleness was attributed to cosmetics–a fashion among young Eastern men. It is hard to imagine the formidably large-bosomed Isobel Burton (1831–1896) passing herself off as an Arab boy, even though she was confident of the success of the disguise she adopted to accompany her headstrong husband on his many absences from his diplomatic duties in Damascus. Passionately devoted to him, she acted as his secretary, rode, swam and fenced with him, and was not prepared to be left behind when he went off on a desert foray. However, in her autobiography *The Romance of Isobel Lady Burton*, she anticipates criticism from readers at home; there is a distinct note of self justification in this passage:

> . . . in our official life we strictly conformed to English customs and conventions; but when we were off duty . . . we used to live a great deal as natives . . . For instance . . . we wore native dress in the desert. I always wore the men's dress on our expeditions in the desert and up the country . . . This is not so dreadful as Mrs Grundy may suppose, as it was all drapery and does not show the figure. There was nothing but the face to show the curious whether you were a man or a woman, and I used to tuck my *kuffiyyah* up to only show my eyes.

Thus attired, she had freedom to go anywhere she liked and to accompany her beloved Richard to all the places which women were not deemed worthy to see, such as Palmyra, the ancient city in central Syria said to have been built by Solomon. One feels, though, that proximity to Richard was her strongest motive:

> I passed at Palmyra as Richard's son; and . . . I soon fell into my part and remembered always to be very respectful . . . Often in my character of a boy I used to run and hold Richard's stirrup as he alighted from his horse, and sat on the edge of his divan while he talked to the Shaykhs of Palmyra.

Naturally there were drawbacks to this marital idyll:

> My chief difficulty was that my toilet always had to be performed in the dead of night. The others never appeared to make any, except in the stream, which was too public for me and I did not wish to appear singular.

Isobel's tone throughout her autobiography is one of dignity. But given any natural scepticism, it is hard sometimes not to envisage an alternative version of events. Here for example she describes her reception in the harem, and attributes the ladies' hysteria to the success of her disguise; but might it not have been mirth at the spectacle of a stout middle-aged lady attempting to pass herself off as a boy?

> In another way my masculine garment had its drawbacks, for I always used to forget that they regarded me as a boy, and I never could remember not to go into the harems. Once or twice I went into them, and the women ran away to hide themselves screaming and laughing at my appearance; and I remember . . . pointing at my chin to plead my youth and also my ignorance of their customs.

Travesty was much more psychologically serious in the case of Isabella Eberhardt who had what amounted to a transference of identity, becoming known as Si Mahmoud and living the life of a desert nomad in North Africa. The mystery of her parentage was undoubtedly a contributory factor. Her mother, Nathalie de Moerder, was the wife of an émigré Russian general settled in Geneva. There she bore him three children, then proceeded to elope with the children's tutor, an Armenian named Trophimowsky. A fourth child Augustin was born and officially recognized by the general as his son, but when Isabella arrived in 1877, neither the general nor Trophimowsky would acknowledge her. She was registered as Eberhardt (her maternal grandmother's name) and given the Christian names Isabella Wilhelmina Marie. In his book *Explorers Extraordinary* John

Women travellers felt they must meet high standards in dress when travelling. May French Sheldon also carried a long blonde wig, and once allowed a powerful native chief, the Mandara of Moschi, to stroke it. The chief had an unpleasant habit of squirting saliva from between his front teeth, and at one audience this fell on the hem of her gown. She was not amused but, unabashed, he asked for her photograph which he added to his collection of European beauties. The locals called her Bebé Bwana (lady boss in Swahili) or Bebé Mzunga (lady white man). When not in a gown Mrs Sheldon wore something appropriate for the palanquin. Her palanquin was much treasured by May French Sheldon. It was when sleeping in the vehicle that she encountered 'the supreme fear of her life', a giant snake which descended from its upper roofing.

Keay refers to the beguiling theory that the poet Rimbaud was her father. He was in Switzerland at the right time, his sister was called Isabella and he owed a debt of loyalty to Queen Wilhemina of the Netherlands. Isabella came to resemble Rimbaud physically and temperamentally–and she claimed that her father died a Muslim, as did Rimbaud.

Always boyish, she developed a real ambivalence about which sex she belonged to; in her journals she referred to herself in both the masculine and the feminine gender. As Si Mahmoud she alternated rigid asceticism with sexual excess. Dressed as a man, selecting and dominating as a man, nevertheless she took male lovers. Much of this can be related to her past in which her love for her brother Augustin played a key part. They were closest in age and united by their desire to escape from the influence of Trophimowsky. Two other siblings had committed suicide; these two romanticized their affections until the relationship grew into an incestuous passion, at any rate on

The man who was her father, and also her tutor, was as ambivalent as Isabelle Eberhardt about her sex, and he pushed her into being photographed as a sailor boy. The other, sad, photograph shows her toothless and syphilitic when she had indeed become an Arab boy.

Isabella's part. By dressing as a man, behaving like a man, she could identify even more strongly with Augustin. Above all, she was clear that the voluptuous, compulsive, often sordid, life she had chosen was the only way:

> I regret nothing and desire nothing. I wait. A nomad with no other homeland than Islam, without family or confidants, alone, forever alone in the solitude of my soul, I will travel my road through life until the time comes for the great eternal sleep of the grave.

She died aged twenty seven. She was ravaged by disease and drugs, but the manner of her death was as freakishly contradictory, yet as rooted in nature, as her life: she was drowned by a desert flood.

Some women travellers adopted disguise for less pleasurably uninhibited reasons, although the results were often as spectacular. May Sheldon (1848–1936) packed evening dress expressly to impress African tribal chiefs, and must have heeded her contemporary Lilias Campbell Davidson's *Hints to Lady Travellers*, although the author was probably envisaging the Scottish Highlands rather than Masai country when she wrote:

> Each dress should have a tray to itself, which should be furnished with tapes on each side to tie the skirt into place

and hold it there. The folding of gowns is an art in itself, and can only be learnt in its higher branches from a lady's maid of experience. Mere words will not describe it.

Englishwomen do not understand the secret of the liberal use of tissue-paper as it is practised by their French sisters. Every fold of a really good dress should have paper placed between it while puffed draperies, sleeves, etc., should be filled with crumpled rolls of the same, which keep them in shape, and altogether prevent creasing.

May Sheldon, the owner of the 'really good dress' destined for the bush, was a wealthy cultured American married to a business man, Eli Lemon Sheldon, and she ran her own publishing firm which printed her translation of Flaubert's *Salammbô* and her novel *Herbert Severance*. Her philosophy expressed in this book, that 'personal independence to a capable woman is a trait no sacrifice is too severe to make secure', perhaps explains why she left her husband in Naples when she set off for Africa in 1891. She intended to travel into Masai country north of Kilimanjaro to study native customs and to collect handicrafts and weapons. She was denounced as mad by local bureaucrats, but she persisted, displaying singularly original methods of getting what she wanted. She travelled in a palanquin carried by Zanzibaris, and invented her own ceremonial robes in order to cut a dash with chieftains. She can have done nothing less, in her curly blonde wig and rhinestone-encrusted ball-dress from which dangled a highly theatrical sword. Her beguiling African nickname was 'Bébé Bwana', and its Parisian music-hall flavour is not entirely misleading.

Amelia Edwards and her companion were more muted spectacles when they visited Cairo in 1873, 'with our hideous palm-leaf hats, green veils and white umbrellas'. One of the first of the British to journey widely in Egypt, Amelia travelled to escape the European climate. She was the daughter of an Army officer, and before her Nile journey wrote only novels and elementary history books. In preparation for the trip she learned as much Egyptology as she could–it was not then a recognized academic subject–and became one of the leading Egyptologists of her age. Her book *A Thousand Miles Up The Nile* (1877) was the record of her extremely adventurous journey. Belonging firmly to the species of Englishwoman who dressed as an Englishwoman abroad, amongst her erudite observations about the ruins and monuments of ancient Egypt other nationalities do not escape her mockery for similar nationalist propensities. She is the mistress of the sartorial put-down: 'Greeks in absurdly stiff white tunics like walking penwipers . . . Armenian priests looking exactly like Portia as the Doctor . . .'

The sense of propriety in dress was an odd source of comfort and strength to the Victorian traveller, and many who adopted more comfortable and appropriate clothes felt as if they had suffered a defeat. Kate Marsden (1859–1931) was a missionary

This was the normal walking costume worn by the American May French Sheldon, whose motto, Noli me tangere, *she carried on a flag attached to her walking staff. In such a subdued outfit, it does seem somewhat doubtful if the warning was heeded.*

who worked among Siberian lepers, enduring extremes of cold. Her autobiographical account *On Sledge and Horseback to the Siberian Lepers* tends from time to time to read like a testimonial to Jaeger. One feels she could endure bizarre outer garments the more easily because of the reassuringly familiar label beneath:

> About the clothing–well, that was a decided burden in more ways than one. I had a whole outfit of Jaeger garments, which I prized more and more as the months went on; then a loose kind of body, lined with flannel, a very thickly-wadded eider-down ulster, with sleeves long enough to cover the hands entirely, the fur collar reaching high enough to cover the head and face. Then a sheep-skin reaching to the feet, and furnished with a collar which came over the fur one. Then over the sheep-skin I had to wear a *dacha*, which is a fur coat of reindeer skin. It was not surprising that, when thus accoutred, broadened, and lengthened by a great many inches, I failed to recognize K.M. in the looking-glass, which a laughing girl held up before me.
>
> But I have not yet finished; some other articles have still to be described. A long thick pair of Jaeger stockings made of long hair; over them a pair of gentlemen's thickest hunting stockings; over them a pair of Russian boots made of felt, coming high up over the knee; and over them a pair of brown felt *valenkies*. Then I was provided with a large fur bag or sack into which I could step; my head-covering was a fur-lined cap, and the et-ceteras consisted of shawls, rugs, and wraps. All this immense load of wool, and fur, and skins to cover a bit of frail and feeble humanity! Yet there was not an ounce too much, as after-experience proved.

Kate Marsden wore this voluminous outfit as she set out for Siberia in 1890 but dressed more conventionally when summoned by Queen Victoria over a decade later to give an account of her travels.

Even after describing vicissitudes that would justify anything as a means of survival, she is apologetic to her readers about the unconventionality of her clothing and defensive about the necessity of riding astride:

> I rather shrink from giving a description of my costume, because it was so inelegant. I wore a jacket, with very long sleeves, and had the badge of the red cross on my left arm. Then I had to wear full trousers to the knees.
>
> The hat was an ordinary deer-stalker, which I had bought in London. I carried a revolver, a whip, and a little travelling bag, slung over the shoulder. I was obliged to ride as a man for several reasons–first because the Yakutsk horses were so wild that it was impossible to ride safely sideways; second, because no woman could ride on a lady's saddle for three thousand versts; third, because, in the absence of roads, the horse has a nasty propensity of stumbling on the stones and amongst the roots of trees, which in these virgin forests make a perfect network, thus precipitating the unfortunate rider

on to the ground; and, fourth, because the horse frequently sinks into the mud up to the rider's feet, and then, recovering its footing, rushes madly along amongst the shrubs and the branches of trees, utterly regardless of the fact that the lady-rider's dress (if she wore one) was being torn into fragments. For these reasons I think no one will blame me for adopting man's mode of riding, and for making adequate provisions by means of the thick leather boots against the probability of bruises, contusions, etc.

It is a surprise to find that Mary Kingsley (1862–1900) is among the inflexible dressers, simply because her perspective on most matters is highly original. The child of a widely travelled inquisitive doctor, she was an extremely clever, initially home-educated girl (but only allowed to teach herself German when she had demonstrated she could starch and iron a shirt properly!). She learned mathematics from a neighbour, and when the family moved to Cambridge she got to know Charles Darwin and T H Huxley. She was only free to travel in 1892, following the death of her parents. Her first voyage, on behalf of the British Museum, was to West Africa to complete her father's collections. In 1894 she accepted a commission from the Natural History Museum to go up the unknown Ogwe River in search of rare fish and plants. Her *Travels in West Africa* was published in 1897 and made her famous. She feared nothing, and was terse

There are few pictures of Mary Kingsley on her travels but we know she dressed conventionally in a good thick skirt, which saved her from injury or worse when she fell into a game pit. She is usually seen in an unprepossessing hat, but in one photograph her hat is quite frivolous.

To get out of a difficult situation, Mary Kingsley once bartered twelve blouses which looked decidedly odd 'when worn by a brawny warrior with nothing else but red paint and a bunch of leopard tails'.

and witty on all subjects, including cannibalism: 'no danger I think to white people, except as to the bother it gives one in preventing one's black companion from being eaten'.

But travelling with these same cannibals, the Fan tribe, in the French Congo, she momentarily loses her humour when she justifies her travelling costume, which seemed to concede nothing to climate or practicality and is the only conventional aspect of this remarkable woman. She fell into a game pit lined with ebony spikes and concludes triumphantly: 'It is at these times you realise the blessings of a good thick skirt. Had I paid heed to the advice of a good many people in England who ought to have known better, and did not do it themselves, and adopted masculine garments, I should have been spiked and done for.'

She also carried an umbrella with which she prodded hippopotami. Indeed, she said 'one had no right to go about Africa in things one would be ashamed of at home.' And she insisted on walking behind her male companion on a jungle path because she knew that the black bootlace with which she had been obliged to do up her stays, was showing through her white blouse in the pouring rain. Finally, she had a strong aversion to trousers and would rather have 'mounted a public scaffold' than have clothed what she preferred to call 'her earthward extremities' in them.

Isabella Bird Bishop (1831–1904) was an English explorer and writer whose original reason for travel was as a cure for

Isabella Bird in the riding habit of her own design.

her delicate health. Courageous, exasperating and extreme ('I do not care for any waterfall but Niagara'), she was the first woman Fellow of the Royal Geographical Society. Usually a model of rectitude, she lost all sense of propriety when she fell in love with a one-eyed desperado named Rocky Mountain Jim. But when *The Times* described her riding gear as 'male habiliments', she wanted the journalist horsewhipped. She had designed the offending garment herself, based on Turkish trousers, and considered it a 'thoroughly serviceable and feminine costume for mountaineering and other rough travelling'. Moreover, even this tasteful outfit was changed for a skirt and she rode side-saddle when she was approaching anything remotely classifiable as civilization.

Some women travellers *had* to take disguise precautions in order to travel at all. Rosita Forbes (1893–1967), who journeyed to Kufara in the heart of the Eastern Sahara in 1920, could not risk detection as a hated infidel. The fierce fanatics of the Libyan deserts would have killed her at once. Her disguise included learning recitations from the *Koran* and metamorphosing herself from a woman 'in a panniered frock with her French hat veiled in drooping lace and high heels to match the rest of her striped cloak . . . into . . . a Bedouin.' She confessed to a pang at leaving her European garments behind in Jedabia, and is wonderfully waspish about her dandified companion

In the frontispiece of one of her books, Rosita Forbes pictures herself in an elegant dress, heavily bejewelled, really the height of fashion. But the photographs inside the book reveal how she went native on a good many occasions.

Once Rosita Forbes reached the suq, she decided that 'we created so much sensation . . . that my grey riding coat and felt hat were out of place.' She sent her man Mustapha 'to discover someone who wished to sell some native clothes. He returned half an hour later [with] the most beautiful white silk jerd, striped like the one I had secretly admired the previous night.' Many of Rosita Forbes's travels in the Sahara were by camel. Sometimes she would cower down on the beast's back so that she was barely distinguishable from burdens of a less human kind.

Alexandra David-Neel with her companion and guide. She wore this 'plain bonnet of Khan' to avoid detection and stained her face with a mixture of cocoa and crushed charcoal. The disguise worked and the Frenchwoman became the first European woman to enter the forbidden city of Lhasa.

Hassanein Bey, who is woefully unable to travel light:

> . . . his suitcase disgorged seven different coloured bottles of eau-de-Cologne and a mass of heterogenous attire more suited to Bond Street than to the Sahara. I had to superintend the packing lest he ignore the claims of malted milk tablets, towels and woollen underclothing in favour of delicately striped shirts and a lavender silk dressing-gown!

Both these unlikely sophisticates were transformed by their arduous desert trek. 'My only European dress had been hidden for months at the bottom of a sack of bully beef tins, yet was I sincere when I echoed Hassanein's vicious "Civilization, Hamdulillah!", as he stuffed his kufiya into a corner of his knapsack and pulled out a fez!'

Alexandra David-Neel (1868–1929) was a French explorer who was also forced to take disguise seriously. She made a series of extraordinary journeys in Central Asia, especially in the high plateaux of Tibet. At the age of fifty-five she disguised herself as a Tibetan beggar woman and was the first European woman to penetrate the forbidden city of Lhasa. In 1923 she records: 'Our code . . . consisted in one single article: *to avoid detection.*' To this end she lengthened her hair with false plaits of jet-black yak's hair, then dyed her own to match with Chinese ink. Her face was stained with a mixture of cocoa and crushed charcoal.

An orientalist and a scholar, Alexandra David-Neel was aged 56 when she went from China to Lhasa. Here she is seen with her companion Lama Yongden (on her right) seated in front of the Potola, or Tibetan 'Vatican'.

'The make-up was rather strange, but suppliers to the theatrical trade . . . have not yet opened branches in the Tibetan wilds.'

She was continually alert for suspicion, and when her headgear attracted comment, judged, 'The time had truly come for the plain bonnet of Khan . . . As soon as I began to wear it all questions and curiosity were at an end.'

In her cliff-hanger (often literally) of a yarn, the bonnet was removed by order in Lhasa itself, her white forehead contrasting with her sunburnt face and terrifying her Tibetan companion: 'You look like a demon . . . I never saw such a face in my life. Everybody will stare at you!'

When Annie Taylor (1855–1920) travelled in Tibet in 1891 she was less exuberant about the need for disguise–as a travelling missionary her thoughts were probably on higher things. The early part of her vocation was spent around the Yangtze River, then near the Tibetan border. She had a great influence on the Chinese women she worked with, initiating Bible Study, the unbinding of feet and the capacity to stand up to their husbands. With the approval of the China Inland Mission, she worked also among the Tibetans: she was the first European woman to penetrate to Tibet–indeed the first European of either sex to do so for fifty years, since the Abbé Huc in the 1840s. One of her converts, a Tibetan youth called Pontso, was her companion on the 2,092 km journey to Tibet, which took them seven months. She had to disguise herself in a small dark hat and baggy sheepskin robes, but perhaps the wide male skirts had a consoling propriety. Her little party crossed the frontier from China in 1892. After Christmas (when she cooked a pudding to celebrate), she cut off her hair so as to pass for a Buddhist nun. Little seems to have ruffled her: during their journey they were ambushed, robbed, attacked by wolves, endured ice and snow, and Annie's horse died under her, but her chief concern was 'claiming the country for the Master'. Unfortunately, her disguise did not save her from discovery, and she was packed off back to China. She finally settled on the border of Sikkim and Tibet, where she distributed Christian tracts to Tibetan traders and became a local character known as *anni*, a Tibetan word for 'aunt'. This description of her by her sister is one of the best evocations of a disguised traveller happily and unselfconsciously at one with her environment:

> Quite low in the valley, while threading my way through the pink pine stems of a wood, I suddenly become aware of an advancing figure that exactly suits the surroundings. A brick-red gown of native cloth with a glimpse of fawn silk at neck and wrists pouched up above the girdle, thus displaying blue cloth trousers tucked into fur boots the shape of night socks, drapes a small person with a merry face, much too fair for a native and topped by a yellow peaked cap. It is my sister!

'The Turkish male dress appeared the only one that could be adopted with delicacy and advantage combined.' This was one explanation given for Lady Hester Stanhope's garb and this portait of her, a posthumous one, is probably reasonably acurate as regards the clothes she was wearing in the early 1800s.

The travelling missionary Annie Taylor also wore disguise in her attempt to penetrate Tibet and convert the inhabitants to Christianity. For the rest of her life, after being expelled from the country, she lives on the border inside China, distributing tracts, although she discarded her robes and resumed her nurse's uniform.

The **THREE FAVORITE AERIAL TRAVELLERS.**

Vincent Lunardi Esq.r first Aeronaut in England.

George Biggin Esq.r

and M.rs Sage first English Female Aerial Traveller.

CHAPTER 8

AVIATRESSES

Laetitia Sage, the first woman to ascend, did not alas have the event captured 'from life' as this, the only engraving, shows Mr Lunardi, the most famous of all balloonists, by her side, which he was not. He had been forced to abandon ship in order to make it 'lighter-than-air'. The other male on board, Colonel Biggin, absent-mindedly forgot the oars. Laetitia consumed at least one bottle of spirits in the comparatively short flight and then dropped the empty bottle overboard.

Over two hundred years ago, the first Englishwoman to fly took to the air as a publicity stunt. In 1785 the Italian balloonist Vincenzo Lunardi had endured several costly failures, one of which earned him this acerbic review in *The Gentleman's Magazine*:

Mr Lunardi ascended, or rather made a feeble attempt to ascend with his balloon after having excited the curiosity of the public to a very high degree by the miracles he intended to perform.

It was obviously necessary to excite public curiosity considerably further for his next attempt. Lunardi's solution was to invite an actress to be airborne. As Sarah Siddons's understudy, Laetitia Sage was probably less than fulfilled in her career, and she jumped at the chance for overnight fame, although not without trepidation at 'the idea that I was daring enough to push myself . . . before my time into the presence of the Deity'.

It was an enormously successful gambit. The crowds were overwhelming as Mrs Sage, Lunardi, and his backer, Colonel George Biggin, met for take-off at St George's Fields on 29 June 1785: 'Beyond a doubt,' said the papers the next day, 'the greatest weight ever sustained by Blackfriar's Bridge was on it yesterday.' However, the balloon refused to rise. Alarmed at the prospect of another fiasco, Lunardi had to lighten the load. Colonel Biggin had been disappointed before and could not be disappointed again. Mrs Sage had been in position for hours and was resolutely determined not to miss her opportunity. Lunardi himself withdrew.

As the balloon rose, Colonel Biggin waved a flag and Mrs Sage blew kisses in all directions. It was not a technically perfect ascent. The Colonel had forgotten the oars, so there was no steering. Thirty miles was claimed as the distance but there were no claims for altitude: Laetitia had broken the barometer soon after take-off. She was an engagingly impractical pioneer (and her instinct to dress for the occasion was echoed as late as 1928, when Lady Mary Heath, flying solo from London to Cape Town, refused to wear trousers, piloting her plane in smart afternoon dress. The plane itself was painted turquoise to match the gemstones in a ring she wore).

All Laetitia Sage's twentieth-century successors share her spirit of determination. It has been hard to narrow the selection of women pilots who are the focus of this chapter: they are a remarkable breed. Like Laetitia, many were motivated to fly by dissatisfaction with their lives, some by deep personal unhappiness. Like her, publicity played a large part in their exploits simply because they were women. Some wooed it, most coped with it, a few were destroyed by it. All were daring, but were not reluctant to confess to fear. They were moved by the aesthetic experience of flying, but not many can express it in writing. There does not seem to be a female Saint-Exupéry. Above all, while competitive, women fliers were fundamentally supportive of each other–they were generous feminists. There were some frivolous and amusing exceptions, but aviatresses were a serious group of individualists, many of whom contributed importantly to the history of aviation. In these modern days of air-traffic control, the excitement of spontaneous decisions and low flying are no longer possible. But travellers by air are true travellers. There are no signposts in the sky to show that a man or woman has been there before; no channels are marked. As Anne Morrow Lindbergh says in *North to the Orient*: 'The flier breaks each second into new uncharted seas.'

Amy Johnson (1903–1941) was motivated to learn to fly by unhappiness. Leaving her home in Hull when hopes of marriage were dashed, she took a job in London, lodging near the London Aeroplane Club. Sir Peter Masefield, who knew her, says that she took the flying lessons she could barely afford as a way out of her misery: 'One of the most elegant ways to commit suicide was to learn to fly.' However, her sadness receded as flying rapidly grew into a passion which dominated the rest of her life. After fifteen hours' tuition she made her first solo flight, and gained her pilot's 'A' Licence in July 1929. By December she had obtained her ground engineer's licence and determined to make a career in aviation.

Sheila Scott (b.1927) found in flying the antidote to an unsatisfactory life. The 'unruly' child of divorced parents, she caught the fever for flight–like many others–at a stunt display. Her sixth birthday treat was going to Sir Alan Cobham's Air Circus and her reaction was prophetic: 'We were gods! It was the most exciting thing I had ever done.'

But it was to be some time before she recaptured the sensation. During the war she was a nurse, disliking the discipline. After the war Alexander Korda, a family friend, gave her a job as 'stand-in' for Deborah Kerr. It was not much of a living. Bit parts in films and TV, a spell in repertory, occasional modelling

An important successor of Laetitia Sage was Mrs Hewlett who took 'an historic step in the emancipation of women' . . . 'for on August 29th she became the first woman to fly solo, on her own Henri Farman, and gain her Royal Aeronautical Club licence.' Later the same year, she taught her son to fly.

jobs–it is hard not to recall Laetitia Sage understudying Sarah Siddons, and not surprising that Sheila Scott should observe, 'Sometimes I felt a deadly boredom with it all.' Six years of an unfortunate marriage and a flirtation with Buddhism preceded her declaration, 'I am going to learn to fly.'

Her first revelation (and a continuing one for fliers) was that the aeroplane was more than a mere machine, that she and it were a partnership. Her instructor told her, with more vividness than elegance: 'Relax and learn to move with the aeroplane as though you were part of it. Please don't clasp the stick as though it's your last possession . . . try and hold it as you would your boyfriend on Saturday night.' After her first solo flight she was back with the gods for the first time since Cobham's Circus: 'I felt [like] a goddess . . . able to extend my vision.'

She won the first races she entered in an old RAF biplane, and in 1960, only a year later, she won the de Havilland Trophy. In 1965 she completed the longest ever solo flight of 31,000 miles

Lady Heath, photographed here as she rose from the cockpit after her return from Cape Town, always wore a smart afternoon dress, and had her aeroplane painted turquoise to match her ring. On this occasion she seems to have compromised by donning a fur.

around the world in 189 flying hours. A woman who had been thoroughly dissatisfied with her life a few years earlier, she was now able to write: 'Flying is the biggest love-affair of my life, full of extremes, of undreamt wonderful things and feelings.'

The Duchess of Bedford also took up flying for emotional reasons. An unconventional duchess, bored with aristocratic drawing-rooms, she learnt to fly in 1926, when she was over sixty. She was naturally solitary and reclusive, a great naturalist and birdwatcher who was happiest leading a rough, isolated life on Barra and Fair Isle. She was, in any case, cut off from human contact and the exchange of ideas by her increasing deafness. As John Duke of Bedford explains in his book *The Flying Duchess*:

> She was now very deaf indeed, suffering from constant buzzing in the ears, but she found that flying and the change in atmospheric pressure brought her miraculous relief ... Although her association with a number of pioneering flights brought her new renown and her final sobriquet of the 'Flying Duchess', the plain fact is that her main reason for spending these long periods in the air was to stop the buzzing in her ears.

She does, nevertheless, deserve a niche in aviation history, for she was a courageous pioneer of long-distance flights. Her

The Duchess of Bedford, pioneer of many long-distance flights, maintained a stiff upper lip in adversity, writing, 'It is rather interesting to experience just how one feels when one knows that the end may come at any moment.' She had never been in an aeroplane until she was 61 years old.

record flight to India in a Fokker with Captain Barnard is well documented in her journal of 1928. As a low-flying naturalist, she clearly had the best of both earth and sky:

> . . . though it is indiscreet to comment on the interest of low flying to one's pilot, who would prefer a clear sky and an altitude of over 7000 feet . . . one is permitted to enjoy oneself in private. What look like spots and patches at 9000 feet become palm-trees and mangrove swamps. One can identify men, dogs, camels, buffaloes and birds, and even the species of the last if they are of conspicuous plumage, like the flamingoes, of which we saw hundreds; storks, cranes, waders and gulls were also disturbed by the mighty insect invading their haunts.

The days of informal flying when pilots landed anywhere–fields, race-courses, golf courses–and animals scurried out of the way, did not last long. Ony a few years later in 1936 Amelia Earhart was to write: 'Now along the airways there's not enough curiosity left for a self-respecting cow even to lift her head to see what goes on in the sky. She's just bored.'

The Duchess of Bedford registered 2,659 hours in the air and completed 200 hours of solo flying. Her death from a flying accident in 1937 was as emotive as her reasons for taking it up. Aged seventy-one, and in a disturbed frame of mind, she took off in her De Havilland Gypsy from Woburn, inexplicably changed her planned course, flew over the open sea and never returned. The verdict on her death remains an open one.

The shade of Laetitia Sage and her publicity stunt hung over the aviatresses. By responding to publicity they acknowledged that they were freaks, exceptions to their sex (whereas most of them were feminist to the core); by not exploiting it they lost the opportunity to finance more flights. Amy Johnson persuaded her family to help her financially in her attempt in 1930

Here seen in conventional pose, the Duchess of Bedford was never a conventional woman, whether hunting, shooting or flying. Her last flight, solo, from which she never returned, was made at the age of 71.

Amy Johnson had not got a natural aptitude for flying but she had great determination and courage.

to fly solo to Australia, but she needed more sponsorship and wrote fruitlessly to innumerable public figures. Eventually a letter to Sir Sefton Brancker, Director of Civil Aviation at the Air Ministry, brought results. He persuaded an oil magnate to share the cost of the aeroplane with the Johnson family and to arrange fuel supplies en route. The epic flight was an extraordinary test for a young woman:

> . . . well out of sight of land . . . forced lower and lower . . . the wind began to blow and the waves rose . . . hemmed in by blackness . . . unable to go on . . . turn back . . . stand still, I circled round and round. I knew that thousands of hungry sharks were waiting . . .

It was the publicity sharks that finally got her. The brouhaha that followed her success gave her a nervous breakdown. Sir Peter Masefield comments that a freelance journalist, William Courtenay (his real name, suitably enough, was Urinowsky), exploited Amy Johnson disgracefully. He engineered her romance with the famous pilot Jim Mollison, and then lived off the unhappy combination. For Amy, the solace of flying had proved to have its own nightmare consequences.

Amelia Earhart (1898–1937) achieved similar instant fame, five years after Charles Lindbergh's epoch-making flight, as the first woman to cross the Atlantic, as passenger and log-keeper. Like Sheila Scott, she had caught flying fever at an exhibition of stunt flying. The pilot went through his tricks, then, to relieve his boredom, swooped down at the public. The public scattered . . . except for Amelia Earhart who stood her ground. The same kind of tenacity saw her through when, helped by her mother, she bought her first aeroplane. It was bright yellow and second-hand:

> The motor was so rough that my feet went to sleep after more than a few minutes on the rudder bar. I had a system of lending the plane for demonstration so as not to be charged storage. Hangar rental would have annihilated my salary.

She was also able to cope very well with the pressures of celebrity. In her book *Last Flight* she amusingly contrasts the reception she received after her solo Atlantic flight in 1932 with her Pacific flight in 1935. Arriving in Ireland in 1932, she had pulled up almost at a farmer's back door. Not knowing the proper phrase for such a situation, she had poked her head out of the cockpit and said, 'I'm from America.' There was no response from the three unimpressed locals. In Oakland, California, in 1935, the reception was tumultuous. She simply records it as: 'At Oakland I did not have to explain whence I came.'

Sheila Scott, who seemed to handle her publicity very skilfully, and was sometimes accused of overdoing it, is quite frank

about her motives. 'My flights cost more money than I ever have.' And there is certainly nothing self-seeking about her account of her arrival after her flight over the North Pole in 1971. There were appalling weather conditions, she had only rudimentary navigational equipment, no radio contact, trouble with her landing gear and finally a nerve-racking landing at Point Barrow with the runway foamed and the crash trucks out. She was so relieved to arrive safely that she forgot the point of her mission:

> I was quite bewildered . . . by dozens of people slapping me on the back, shaking my hand, taking pictures and all chattering at once. I had almost forgotten the Pole.

Like Amelia Earhart, she was in charge of her own celebrity. Temperamentally she could never have been swamped by fame like Amy Johnson, but there is a certain wistfulness after her longest solo flight round the world in 1964:

> A kaleidoscope of waiting friends, flowers, customs officers, cameras, mikes–look here–look there, being so tired–oh so tired, but unable to relax . . .

Jean Batten (b.1909), who cut Amy Johnson's solo record to Australia by four days in 1934, found a way of dealing with the ephemeral nature of her life:

How bitter-sweet it all was . . . flying about the world, visiting these great cities, meeting many people, making many friends, then having to fly off again. I consoled myself with the thought that I always saw the very best side of everything, and seldom stayed long enough in one place to have any illusions or ideals shattered.

Women fliers incline to a breathless, girlish quality describing some of the most fearsome moments in their memoirs, but there is no doubt of the uncertainties and terrors they overcame, however *Girls' Own* the style. Pauline Gower (1910–1946) learned to fly before she was twenty and was the first woman in England to get her commercial licence, which she did in 1931. She became a highly professional career flier who commanded the women's division of the Air Transport Auxiliary during the war. These women pilots prided themselves on having a slightly better air-safety record than their male counterparts, so it is ironic to read Pauline Gower's early recollections of erratic flying. Acquiring the necessary 100 hours for a 'B' licence, she knew very little about navigation 'and did not even know how a compass worked'. Amy Johnson invited Pauline Gower and her friend and co-pilot Dorothy Spicer to Paris for a meeting of the International League of Aviators–and lent them one of her planes. They were the first English girls to fly to France but there were various mishaps, as Pauline Gower recalls:

Pauline Gower was the first English woman to hold a commercial flying licence, which she obtained in 1931. She went on to command the women's division of the band of fliers who ferried war planes in 1939–1945. But she disliked the name 'ATA girls'.

In great distress I called through the earphones: 'Dorothy, the throttle's bust! What shall we do?' Dorothy's voice came back, cheerfully reassuring: 'No it isn't, you chump'; I've only got a suitcase on it!'

They amused themselves by swooping past and diving upon any ship or fishing smack beneath them–'the manoeuvre being accompanied by inaudible shrieks of mirth from us'. On their return in bad weather they kept course as far as Mons, but 'at this juncture Dorothy let her map blow away.

'"Pauline," she called to me through the speaking tube, "can I have your map? Mine's blown away."

'I handed mine back to her but in some unaccountable way my hand missed hers, and before we knew what had happened, my map had followed hers, fluttering hundreds of feet below. So there we were, flying over totally strange country with no map to guide us.' They arrived, out of petrol, at Brussels ('Dorothy pulled off a very creditable dead-stick landing,') . . . which turned out to be Liège.

Jean Batten possessed similar intrepidity but rather more practicality. In 1933 she set out to fly solo to Australia, but crashed near Karachi and had to ship the damaged plane back to England. Her second attempt–in a plane once owned by the Prince of Wales–was sabotaged when it broke down in Rome and had to be flown back to London for an overhaul. She kept

Jean Batten, the long-distance flier, beat Amy Johnson's record time to Australia but, like other aviatresses, was overcome by feelings of loneliness.

her head, despite these nerve-racking and very public failures, and on her third attempt succeeded in beating Amy Johnson's solo record. In 1935 she flew the South Atlantic from Dakar to Natal in Brazil, 1,281 miles in a land plane that had no radio. No woman had made this crossing solo, though Anne Morrow Lindbergh had been her husband's co-pilot from Africa to South America. Jean Batten describes the problem of keeping a pessimistic imagination at bay in her book *My Life*.

> I became overwhelmed by the intense feeling of loneliness which only the long-distance flier knows, and found myself listening intently to the rhythmic beat of the engine and trying not to think what the consequences of an engine failure now would mean . . .

While Amelia Earhart could write, 'Of course no pilot sits and feels his pulse as he flies. He has to be part of the machine,' she too was prey to the fear and loneliness of the long-distance flier on her solo Atlantic flight in 1932:

> Looking back, there are less cheering recollections of that night over the Atlantic. Of seeing, for instance, the flames lick through the exhaust collector ring, and wondering, in a detached way, whether one would prefer drowning to incineration. Of the five hours of storm during black midnight

when I kept right side up by instruments alone, buffeted about as I never was before. Of much beside, not least the feeling of loneliness and of realisation that the machine I rode was doing its best and required from me the best I had.

It was perhaps easier for the Duchess of Bedford to maintain the stiffest of upper lips, having already lived a long life, and always being ready to be distracted by the view below. This entry is from her journal of the record long-distance Cape flight in 1930 when the oil gauge 'had gone on strike and was giving quite needless anxiety' as they flew over Lake Victoria:

> It is rather interesting to experience just how one feels when one knows that the end may come at any moment. My own experience is that with a little determination panic can be lived down . . . it is possible to divert the thoughts to other channels and accept 'Che Sara Sara'. It is the more easy if there is as much to interest oneself in as there was on this occasion.

The view was obviously a compensation for the risk, as is confirmed by Amelia Earhart writing of her 1935 flight from Hawaii to California:

> After midnight the moon set and I was alone with the stars. I have often said that the lure of flying is the lure of beauty, and I need no other flight to convince me that the reason flyers fly, whether they know it or not, is the aesthetic appeal of flying.

Anne Morrow Lindbergh, while capable of magic-carpet lyricism herself, was stern about the practicalities that made it possible:

> There is always a back stairs to magic and it is just as well to keep it in mind . . . The back stairs of aviation magic is sometimes a parachute and sometimes a rubber lifeboat. But it can also be a radio tube or a sextant or a life preserver or snake-bite serum or a bug-proof tent or a revolver or a compass–or even a pair of heavy boots. One must always be thinking, not only 'Thirteen hours of gasoline will take us to Aklavik', but also, 'If we have an engine failure on the way, we have food enough for thirty days' walking to an outpost'.

But it must be pointed out that Amelia Earhart, obviously discounting the possibility of walking on the water, flew the Atlantic with only a thermos of hot soup . . .

If anything united this group of individualists it was feminism. As soon as she made her name with the Australia flight, Jean Batten realized the impossibility of combining marriage with the work she wanted to do:

Before leaving England I had become engaged, but on arrival in Australia realized I should have to choose between matrimony and my career . . . Now that I had tasted the fruits of success and felt the urge to rise to even greater heights, any responsibility, however light, that would in any way hinder or deter my progress was not to be considered. In short, I suppose ambition claimed me and I considered no sacrifice too great to achieve the task I had set myself.

Her independence made her able to confront officialdom head-on, and win. On her solo flight from England to New Zealand in 1936 the aeroplane's tyre blew out at Timor, a Portuguese island north of Australia. There was a long delay until someone had the bright idea of stuffing the tyre with sponges, and Jean Batten was able to fly on to Australia for more sophisticated repairs. There officials tried to dissuade her from the last leg of her flight, 1,200 nautical miles across the Tasman Sea to her native New Zealand. She insisted on going, and took the wind out of their bureaucratic sails by adding that if she went missing no Australian Government money was to be spent on a sea search. She became the first woman to fly alone to New Zealand, and created a new record for a pilot of either sex: from Great Britain in 5 days 21 hours and 30 minutes.

Pauline Gower disliked the nickname 'Ata-girls' for her select division of the ATA. 'It was not easy at first, nor in fact has it ever been easy–this life we have chosen. No one would take us seriously.' There were only eight women in the division at first–she insisted they were not referred to as 'girls'–but by the end of the war there were more than a hundred, from most Allied countries. All 'glamour' treatment from the press was rejected. No special treatment was demanded by the women, and Pauline Gower saw that they were paid the same as the men of ATA. She herself flew different aircraft including Lancasters, Hurricanes, Mosquitoes and Spitfires.

Amy Johnson joined the ATA without fuss and as part of the team. Her vast experience was never foisted on anyone, and her advice only offered when it was solicited. On 5 January 1941 she was delivering a plane in bad weather when she ran out of fuel. She bailed out into the icy, rough waters of the Thames Estuary. HMS *Hazlemere* was nearby and the captain dived in to save her. Both were drowned.

Amy Johnson's short life was undoubtedly the unhappier for the attentions of the press, who treated her as a sort of performing bear. It was the press who tried to preserve a 'feminine' archness in their interviews with the women pilots, which was quite at odds with their true natures. Anne Morrow Lindbergh took umbrage when quizzed by journalists about her aerial housekeeping:

I feel slightly insulted. Over in the corner my husband is being asked vital masculine questions, clean-cut steely technicalities

or broad abstractions. But I am asked about clothes and lunch-boxes . . .

In 1932, a group of aviatresses got together for a Women's Flying Meeting at Atlantic Park, Eastleigh, near Southampton. They included Amy Johnson so Jim Mollison came along too.

But there were always frivolous (and likeable) exceptions prepared to play ball with the expectations of the press. Violette de Sibour, the heiress daughter of Gordon Selfridge, flew 10,000 miles on a ten-month trip to Indo-China with her husband Jacques. The purpose of their trip was to go big-game hunting; their plane was named *Safari* which, Violette gaily explained, 'generally means a trip into the blue.' She did not help the image of the serious women career pilots when she wrote, 'Oh, the joy of shedding one's oily clothes, having a luxurious bath, and finally appearing in complete evening attire–diamond earrings and all.'

Although she complained, 'This flying business is terribly tiring,' her social stamina is inexhaustible:

Tehran proved to be the most hospitable city in the world. We were invited by the French legation to lunch and the British legation to dinner on the same day.

In her breathless narrative, they reach India, Jacques is sick in the Ganges after a night out, they fly off to Gaya and, failing to find the aerodrome, make an emergency landing in a sandriver. The natives who witnessed this spectacular arrival assumed mob proportions, endangering the aeroplane in their desire to inspect it closely. Violette showed sterling courage in defence of their machine, but it is the loss of her wardrobe she mourns most deeply:

Gordon Selfridge, founder of the famous emporium in Oxford Street, London, had strong connections with flying. His daughter Violette was no mean traveller, and in the shop he sold not only small aeroplanes but flying gear and accessories. Here is a group of his 'girls' showing off their leather flying suits in the late 1920s or early 1930s. It was not the kind of gear that appealed to daughter Violette. She wrote: 'For the interest of other women planning to take similar adventures, I will give a list of what I took:

1 complete Beige sport suit consisting of skirt, sweater and sweater coat.
A sleeveless Beige summer frock and wide brimmed felt hat.
A black lace evening dress and black fringed shawl.
Two pairs of shoes and one pair of silver slippers.
Two complete sets of lingerie and half a dozen pairs of silk stockings.'

In desperation, I seized a stick from one astonished old man and laid about me. They must have thought this was something new in the line of 'memsahibs'. But as the night deepened the crowd grew even thicker. They stole my gloves, my glasses and my hat.

But on the whole the experiences of women fliers encouraged them to become ambassadresses of equality. Sheila Scott sees flying as 'an almost complete fulfilment, providing a vision of a world friendship without prejudice'. Amelia Earhart, meeting disadvantaged Mexican women, wrote: 'I . . . hope for the day when women will know no restrictions . . . but will be individuals free to live their lives as men are free.' Indeed, she felt it her mission to encourage all other women to greater independence of thought and action. In his *Book of Famous Fliers*, it is incredible that Jim Mollison titles the chapter on Amelia Earhart, 'The Woman Lindbergh': he sees her merely as the female version of quite another pilot. She was luckier in her husband, whom she felt found 'a grim satisfaction' in 'being for once the male left behind while the female fares forth adventure-bound'. It was to him that she wrote the letter explaining the reason for her final flight, and providing an inspiration for the women who followed her:

Women must try to do things as men have tried. When they fail, their failure must be but a challenge to others.

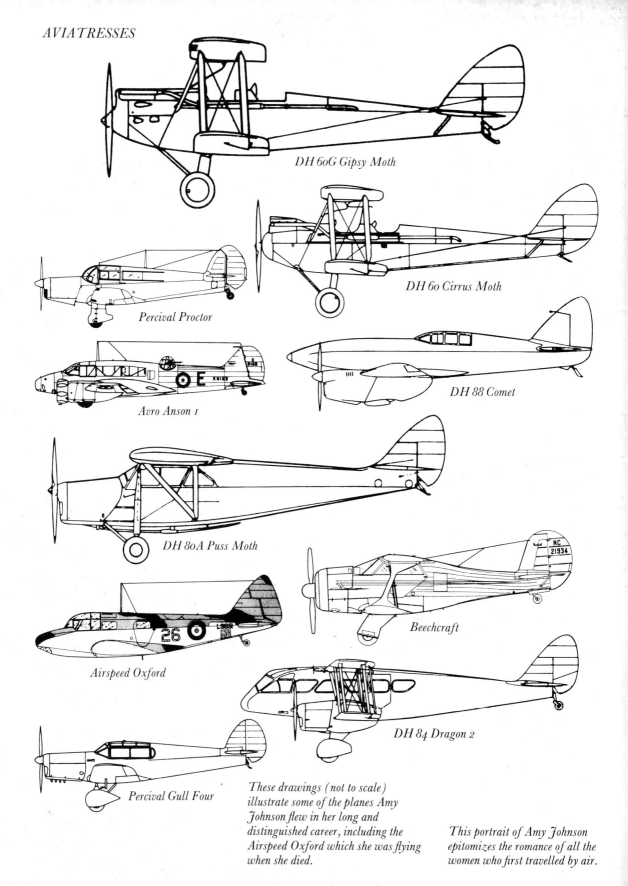

DH 60G Gipsy Moth

DH 60 Cirrus Moth

Percival Proctor

DH 88 Comet

Avro Anson 1

DH 80A Puss Moth

Beechcraft

Airspeed Oxford

DH 84 Dragon 2

Percival Gull Four

These drawings (not to scale)
illustrate some of the planes Amy
Johnson flew in her long and
distinguished career, including the
Airspeed Oxford which she was flying
when she died.

This portrait of Amy Johnson
epitomizes the romance of all the
women who first travelled by air.

SELECT BIBLIOGRAPHY

Chapter 1: *Climbers*

DAVID-NEEL, ALEXANDRA, *With Mystics and Magicians in Tibet* (John Lane, 1931)

DAVID-NEEL, ALEXANDRA, *My Journey to Lhasa* (Heinemann, 1927)

DU FAUR, FREDA, *The Conquest of Mount Cook* (Allen & Unwin, 1915)

HAVERGAL, FRANCIS RIDLEY, *Swiss Letters* (James Nisbet & Co, 1881)

LE BLOND, ELIZABETH, *Day In Day Out* (John Lane, The Bodley Head, 1928)

LE BLOND, ELIZABETH, *The High Alps in Winter* (Sampson Low, 1883)

LE BLOND, ELIZABETH, *The Story of an Alpine Winter* (Bell, 1907)

MATTHEWS, C. E., *The Annals of Mont Blanc* (Fisher Unwin, 1898)

MILLER, LUREE, *On Top of the World* (Paddington Press, 1976)

PECK, ANNIE, *High Mountain Climbing in Peru & Bolivia* (Fisher Unwin, 1912)

UNDERHILL, MIRIAM, *Give Me the Hills* (Methuen & Co, 1956)

WILLIAMS, CICELY, *Women on the Rope* (Allen & Unwin, 1973)

WORKMAN, FANNY BULLOCK and WILLIAM HUNTER, *The Call of the Snowy Hispar* (Constable, 1910)

WORKMAN, FANNY BULLOCK and WILLIAM HUNTER, *Ice-bound Heights of the Mustagh* (Constable, 1908)

WORKMAN, FANNY BULLOCK and WILLIAM HUNTER, *Peaks and Glaciers of Nun Kun* (Constable, 1909)

WORKMAN, FANNY BULLOCK and WILLIAM HUNTER, *Two Summers in the Ice-Wilds of Eastern Karakoram* (Fisher Unwin, 1917)

Chapter 2: *Actresses, Divas and Dancers*

BEAUVALLET, LEON, *Rachel and the New World* (London, 1967)

BERNHARDT, SARAH, *My Double Life* (Heinemann, 1907)

BOLITHO, WILLIAM, *Twelve Against the Gods* (Heinemann, 1930)

BULMAN, JOAN, *Jenny Lind* (Barrie, 1956)

DANDRE, V., *Anna Pavlova in Art and Life* (Cassell, 1932)

DUMESNIL, *Amazing Journey* (Paris, 1823)

DUNCAN, ISADORA, *The Art of the Dance* ed. S. Cherry (Theatre Art Books, 1969)

DUNCAN and MACDOUGAL, *Isadora Duncan's Russian Days* (Gollancz, 1929)

DUNCAN, ISADORA, *My Life* (Gollancz, 1928)

FARSON, DANIEL, *Marie Lloyd and Music Hall* (Stacey, 1972)

JACOBS, N., *'Our Marie': a Biography* (London, 1936)

KERENSKY, OLEG, *Anna Pavlova* (Hamish Hamilton, 1973)

KLEIN, H., *The Reign of Patti* (Da Capo Press, 1978)

KNEPLER, HENRY, *The Gilded Stage* (Constable, 1968)

MARINACCI, BARBARA, *Leading Ladies* (Redman, 1962)

MELBA, NELLIE, *Melodies and Memories* (Thornton Butterworth, 1925)

MONTEZ, LOLA, *Lectures and Autobiography* (London, 1858)

MURPHY, AGNES, G., *Melba: a Biography* (Chatto and Windus, 1909)

PAVLOVA, ANNA (trans. Sebastien Voirol), *Pages of My Life* (Henry Holt, New York, 1947)

RAVEN, SUSAN and WEIR, ALISON, *Women in History* (Weidenfeld & Nicolson, 1981)

RICHARDSON, JOANNA, *Rachel: a Biography* (Max Reinhart, London, 1956)

SARGEANT, PHILIP WALSINGHAM, *Dominant Women* (Books for Libraries Press, 1969)

SCHNEIDER, ILYA ILYITCH, *Isadora Duncan (The Russian Years)* (Macdonald, 1968)

SCOTT-HOLLAND, H., and ROCKSTRO, W. S., *Memoir of Mme Jenny Lind-Goldsmidt* (John Murray, 1891)

SILVER, NATHAN, *Lost New York* (Houghton Mifflin, 1966)

STIER, THEODORE, *With Pavlova Around the World* (Hurst & Blackett, London 1927)

SVETLOV, VALERIAN, *Anna Pavlova* (Dover Books, New York, 1975)

TREASE, GEOFFREY, *Seven Stages* (Heinemann, 1964)

WYNDHAM, H., *The Magnificent Montez* (Hutchinson, 1935)

Chapter 3: *Missionaries*

ACRES, LOUIS, *Helen Hanson: a Memoir* (Allenson, 1928)

CAREY, WILLIAM, *Travel and Adventure in Tibet* (Hodder & Stoughton, 1902)

LIVINGSTONE, W. P., *Mary Slessor of Calabar* (Hodder & Stoughton, 1918)

MABEL, E., and MAJOR, F., *On the Wings of a Wish* (Church Missionary Society, 1908)

MARSDEN, KATE, *On Sledge and Horseback to Outcast Siberian Lepers* (1893)

MIDDLETON, DOROTHY, *Victorian Lady Travellers* (Routledge & Kegan Paul, 1965)

MOFFAT, J. S., *Lives of Robert and Mary Moffat* (Fisher Unwin, 1886)

SEAVER, GEORGE, *David Livingstone, His Life and Letters* (Lutterworth, 1957)

SLESSOR, MARY, *Our Faithful God: Answers to Prayer* (privately published)

STREATFIELD, HENRIETTA S., *Glimpses of Indian Life* (Marshall Brothers, 1908)

SELECT BIBLIOGRAPHY

Chapter 4: *Huntresses*

BAILLIE MRS W. W., *Days and Nights of Shikar* (The Bodley Head, 1921)

BLIXEN, KAREN, *Letters* (Weidenfeld & Nicolson, 1981)

BLIXEN, KAREN, *Out of Africa* (Penguin, 1954)

DUNCAN, JANE, *A Summer Ride in Tibet* (Collins, 1906)

HAWKINS, R. E., *Jim Corbett's India* (Oxford University Press, 1978)

HERBERT, AGNES, *Two Dianas in Somaliland* (The Bodley Head, 1908)

HUXLEY, ELSPETH, *Flame Trees of Thika* (Chatto, 1959)

HUXLEY, ELSPETH, *The Mottled Lizard* (Chatto, 1962)

JENKINS, LADY, *Sport and Travel in Both Tibets* (Blades, East & Blades, 1910)

JOHNSON, MARTIN, *Camera Trails in Africa* (George Allen & Unwin, 1924)

JOHNSON, MARTIN, *Safari* (G P Putnam's Sons, 1928)

JOHNSON, OSA, *Four Years in Paradise* (Hutchinson & Co., 1942)

MARKHAM, BERYL, *West with the Night* (Virago, 1984)

PAKENHAM, VALERIE, *The Noonday Sun* (Methuen & Co, 1985)

SMYTHIES, OLIVE, *Tiger Lady* (Heinemann, 1953)

Chapter 5: *Governesses*

ANON, The Private Governess (The Literary Souvenir, 1826)

ANON, Recollections of a Royal Governess (Hutchinson, 1915)

BICKNELL, ANNA L., *Life in the Tuileries Under the Second Empire* (Fisher Unwin, 1895)

BRUNEL, ROSAMUND GOTCH, *Maria, Lady Callcott* (John Murray, 1937)

CALLCOTT, LADY MARIA, *Journal of a Residence in Chile* (Longman and John Murray, 1824)

CALLCOTT, LADY MARIA, *Journal of a Voyage to Brazil* (Longman and John Murray, 1824)

EAGAR, M., *Six Years at the Russian Court* (Hurst & Blackett, 1906)

FIELD, RACHEL, *All This and Heaven Too* (Collins, 1939)

HOWE, BEA, *A Galaxy of Governesses* (Verschoyle, 1954)

LEONOWENS, ANNA, *Siamese Harem Life* (Arthur Barker, 1952)

LOTT, EMMELINE, *English Governesses in Egypt* (2 volumes), (Bentley, 1866)

NEETON, MISS, *Journal of a Governess* (2 volumes), Oxford University Press, 1937)

PERCIVAL, ALICE, *The English Miss* (Harrap, 1939)

PERCIVAL, ALICE, *The English Miss Today and Yesterday* (Harrap, 1939)

PITCHER, HARVEY, *When Miss Emmie Was in Russia* (Century, 1984)

Chapter 6: *Memsahibs*

BARR, PAT, *The Memsahibs* (Secker & Warburg, 1976)

DIVER, MAUD, *The Englishwoman in India* (John Murray, 1936)

DIVER, MAUD, *Honoria Lawrence* (John Murray, 1936)

DUNBAR, JANET, *Golden Interlude* (John Murray, 1955)

EDEN EMILY, *Up the Country* (abridged version, Oxford University Press, 1930)

FAY, ELIZA, *Original Letters from India 1779–1815* Introduction by E. M. Forster, (Hogarth Press, 1925)

HICKEY, WILLIAM, *Memoirs 1749–1790* (Hurst & Blackett, 1919)

MORRIS, JAMES, *Farewell the Trumpets* (Faber & Faber, 1978)

PARKES, FANNY, *Wanderings of a Pilgrim in Search of the Picturesque* (London, 1850)

PEMBLE, JOHN (ed.), *Miss Fane in India* (Alan Sutton, 1985)

POWELL, VIOLET, *Flora Annie Steel* (Heinemann, 1981)

SITWELL, CONSTANCE, *Flowers and Elephants* (Jonathan Cape, 1929)

STANFORD, J. K., *Ladies in the Sun* (Alley Press, 1962)

STEEL, FLORA ANNIE, *The Complete Indian Housekeeper and Cook* (Heinemann, 1888)

STREATFIELD, HENRIETTA S., *Glimpses of Indian Life* (1908)

Chapter 7: *Masqueraders*

BIRD BISHOP, ISABELLA, *A Lady's Life in the Rocky Mountains* (London, 1879)

BLANCH, LESLEY, *The Wilder Shores of Love* (John Murray, 1954)

BLUNT, LADY ANNE, *Bedouin Tribes of the Euphrates* (John Murray, 1879)

BLUNT, LADY ANNE, *Pilgramage to the Nedj* (John Murray, 1881)

BURTON, ISOBEL, *The Romance of Isobel, Lady Burton* (Hutchinson, 1897)

CAMPBELL DAVIDSON, LILIAN, *Hints to Lady Travellers* (London, 1889)

DAVID-NEEL, ALEXANDRA, *My Journey to Lhasa* (Heinemann, 1927)

DAVID-NEEL, ALEXANDRA, *With Mystics and Magicians in Tibet* (John Lane, 1931)

FOX SCHMIDT, MARGARET, *Passion's Child* (Hamish Hamilton, 1977)

KEAY, JOHN, *Explorers Extraordinary* (John Murray, 1985)

KINGSLEY, MARY, *Travels in West Africa* (Macmillan, 1897)

KINGSLEY, MARY, *West Arfrican Studies* (Macmillan, 1899)

MARSDEN, KATE, *On Sledge and Horseback to Outcast Siberian Lepers* (Record Press, 1893)

MERYON, C. L.. *Memoirs of Lady Hester Stanhope* (Henry Colburn, 1845)

MIDDLETON, DOROTHY, *Victorian Lady Travellers* (Routledge & Kegan Paul, 1965)

MONTAGU, LADY MARY WORTLEY, Letters 1763

MONTAGU, LADY MARY WORTLEY, Letters 1837 (Philadelphia: Carey Lea Blanchard)

SILK BUCKINGHAM, JAMES, *Travels in Mespotamia* (Colburn, 1827)

STEPHEN, R., *The Destiny of Isabella Eberhardt* (London, 1951)

TAYLOR, ANNIE R., Diary (included in William Cary's *Travel and Adventure in Tibet*) (Hodder & Stoughton, 1902)

Chapter 8: *Aviatresses*

BATTEN, JEAN, *My Life* (Harrap, 1938)

BEDFORD, JOHN, DUKE OF, *The Flying Duchess* (Macdonald, 1968)

SELECT BIBLIOGRAPHY

DAVID, B., *Amelia Earhart* (1977)

GARDINER, LESLIE, *Man in the Clouds* (Constable, 1963)

GOWER, PAULINE, *Women with Wings* (John Long, 1938)

LINDBERG, ANNE MORROW, *Listen! the Wind* (Chatto & Windus, 1938)

LINDBERG, ANNE MORROW, *North to the Orient* (Harcourt Brace, 1938)

MAY, CHARLES PAUL, *Women in Aeronautics* (Nelson, 1962)

MOLLISON, J. A. (ed.), *The Book of Famous Flyers: an Interesting Account of the History of Aviation from the early Pioneers to Present-Day Aces of the Air* (Collins & Sons, 1936)

SCOTT, SHEILA, *On Top of the World* (Hodder & Stoughton, 1973)

SIBOUR, VIOLETTE DE, *Flying Gypsies* (Putnam, 1930)

WELCH, ANN, *Happy to Fly: an Autobiography* (John Murray, 1983)

INDEX